design & make
scarves, collars, ties & belts

Colourful selection of ties and belts to make (see Chapters 4, 5, 7, 11).

design & make

scarves, collars, ties & belts

CHRISTINA BRODIE

A & C BLACK

For fashionistas everywhere

DISCLAIMER
Everything written in this book is to the best of my knowledge true, and every effort has been made to ensure accuracy and safety, but neither author nor publisher can be held responsible for any resulting injury, damage or loss to either persons or property. Any further information which will assist in updating any future editions would be gratefully received. Read through all the information in each chapter before commencing work. Follow all health and safety guidelines and where necessary obtain health and safety information from the suppliers.

First published in Great Britain 2009
A&C Black Publishers
36 Soho Square
London W1D 3QY
www.acblack.com

ISBN 978-0-7136-8834-4

CIP catalogue records for this book are available from the British Library and the US Library of Congress.

Book design: Penny Mills and Sutchinda Thompson
Cover design: Sutchinda Thompson
Commissioning Editor: Susan James
Managing Editor: Sophie Page
Copy Editor: Carol Waters
Proofreader: Julian Beecroft

Printed and bound in China

contents

1 introduction

This book attempts to explore and demonstrate the ease of making stylish, wearable, modern accessories using a variety of materials. The focus of the book is on items that can be relatively easily made at home, and mostly from soft fabrics, although a couple of items require the use of leather pieces. Some will only take a few hours to make with minimal sewing input and materials; others will take somewhat longer and demand more patience, experience and handsewing skills. Some are designed for everyday or seasonal use; others as one-off or 'special occasion' items. Most are not difficult to make (being quicker to make than a cross-stitch sampler or a quilt, and wearable besides!). Simple, effective and practical pattern construction and designing is covered later in the book for those who would like an additional challenge and the opportunity to make a 'bespoke' item using the wearer's exact measurements (see chapter 14).

I do not provide patterns for every item, since some use a basic rectangular strip as their pattern, and as such their dimensions can be measured directly onto the fabric. Where I do provide patterns, these can be found in the section on Patterns, towards the end of the book. Patterns drawn on a grid should be scaled up. The sides of each large square within the grid equal 5 cm (2 in.). Elsewhere, the patterns of smaller items, too simple or complicated to be scaled up using a grid, are displayed with dimensions added.

I have tried to include a varied range of projects which cover a set of skills and making techniques. I have aimed to make the items in this book as 'current' as I possibly can, but also with the anticipation that some, at least, will remain stylish and wearable for years to come. I hope that the book will provide an interesting introduction to techniques for complete beginners and those with less sewing experience, as well as providing fresh inspiration to more experienced individuals and young fashion students.

I would like to thank Susan James, of A & C Black, for her support and enthusiasm for the project; all those who have offered me continued encouragement; and lastly, the suppliers of the various materials used in this book, without which it would certainly not have been possible.

Christina Brodie
May 2008

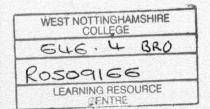

opposite: Different colours, textures and material types provide inspiration for making a wide range of accessories.

2 materials and techniques

Over the following pages are described a selection of the materials used in this book. With the exception of the leather that I specify for buckle straps (I find it unbeatable as regards fitness for purpose), don't necessarily feel bound by these; they represent suggestions for materials that I felt interpreted the patterns best, and they may well not be available to you. A huge variety of fabrics can be used for the types of accessories shown in this book. They are not subject to some of the considerations needed for accessories that are likely to receive a lot of hard wear and tear: for example, the load-bearing capacities and strength of fabric that have to be considered when designing for bags do not apply here.

I don't specify quantities of fabric in the lists of materials at the beginning of each chapter. This is for the simple reason that your choice of fabric may be different to mine, and may be a different width to mine. The most important thing to bear

in mind is whether all the pattern pieces fit onto the piece of fabric, and whether their grain orientation is correct. Because several of the items in this book are made using a simple rectangular strip of fabric, patterns are not always necessary, but it is still advisable to ensure you have sufficient fabric. Where patterns are shown at the beginning of each chapter, trace them off or scale them up before marking them with all relevant information (chapter 14), and take them with you when shopping for fabrics.

A note on buying quantities of fabric and materials: many suppliers will only sell lengths of fabric in a minimum quantity. It is generally rather galling when considerable amounts of fabric are left at the end of a project, although prudent to overbuy on occasion (for example, fabric pieces may need to be re-cut if mistakes have been made). Try to identify several projects that you would like to make from the book, or design your-

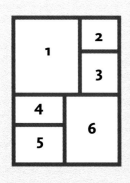

1   Benares brocades of different colours.
2   Polka-dot print lightweight polycotton.
3   Trim.
4   Feather trims.
5   Silk habotai and a variety of acetate linings.
6   The front and reverse of a piece of double-sided tie-silk fabric.

self, to use up the excess materials; or, alternatively, make several of the same item!

Lighter-weight fabrics that cannot hold a shape well on their own will need to be strengthened with a fusible fabric or other stiffening or support fabric. I recommend a firm but lightweight fusible such as Vilene® for lightweight fabrics. A heavier fusible drill may be suitable for medium-weight fabrics, but for accessories of this size it is generally not necessary, and I do not use it in this book. Denims and heavier fabrics need much less support; the denim belt in chapter 4 is self-supporting as it has sufficient stiffness to hold a strong shape. You will see me refer variously to support fabrics as fusibles, stiffeners or stiffening fabrics, but effectively they mean the same thing.

Many of the materials in this book are easy to work with. They can be broken down into several categories:

FABRICS (WOVENS):

Silk satin – this is a very fine and soft satin-weave fabric which is suitable for lining. It works best visually and shifts around less when given some support, such as an underlay of wadding. Because the top surface is so smooth and shiny due to the satin weave, it also marks and snags easily; therefore it is essential to keep hands scrupulously clean and handle the fabric with care.

Tie silk – this is available in many different colours and weights. It may be either single-sided or double-sided and is not usually of a very generous width. That having been said, the best tie silks are spectacular; some are double-sided, with a different design on both sides, therefore opening up a wide range of possibilities. They are easy to sew, generally fairly stable fabrics, and the reflective quality of the silk emphasizes their jewel-like colours.

Wool fabrics – the best wool fabrics have a soft and non-scratchy quality. Pay attention to their other qualities, too, such as the elasticity of the weave and the way in which that can impact upon design potential. One of the projects in this book, the Pompom Scarf (chapter 6) was made from a soft wool fabric resembling tweed, but with a much looser weave. Most woollen fabrics are wonderfully easy to sew: sewing-machine needles go through them like a knife through butter.

Cottons – my favourite from this group of fabrics are traditional Indian printed or ethnic cottons, which may often incorporate hand-printed elements. The genuine articles have a richness of colour and pattern that cannot be found anywhere else.

Depending on their finish, cottons can have a shiny or matt appearance, and be very crisp or quite a lot softer. I prefer a 'natural' look and soft feel, particularly for scarves; the rough feel that can come from some cotton fabrics is unpleasant around the neck. A softer handle and appearance is more pleasing to sight and touch, and less likely to show up marks. Denim is made using a twill weave and therefore is very compact and hard-wearing, and thus good for items such as belts; it is unlikely to need additional stiffening from fusible fabrics as it has a natural inherent stiffness and ability to hold a shape.

Synthetics – these can include mixtures of natural and synthetic fibres such as cotton polyesters, where a small amount of synthetic fibre is added to a mixture of natural fibres to improve handle, fit, stretch or care. Fabric technology is such nowadays that fabrics may contain up to five different types of fibre, each imparting their own quality to the fabric.

Benares brocade is popularly used for saris, woven from silk and metallic-coated viscose. For obvious reasons, it should be ironed on as low a setting as possible. I also prefer to protect the iron plate and fabric with a sheet of paper

Assortment of denims.

placed between the iron and the fabric. Benares brocade comes in a wide range of colours, usually one bright colour with a gold or silver metallic pattern. Where border patterns are woven along the length of the brocade, the fabric is intended to be cut up to produce several rolls of edging fabric.

Linings – lightweight linings work well in certain situations. The Folded Silk Tie (see chapter 11) uses a silk habotai lining. Silk satin, in conjunction with a support fabric such as Quiltex®, can also work well (see Faux Fur Wrap, chapter 13). Acetate linings are good for general-purpose use. It is not always necessary to line an accessory; some accessories can be backed with self-fabric (Eyelet Belt, chapter 4) or the pattern can be folded back on itself and behind the stiffener to create a self-fabric back (Polka Dot Collar, chapter 10).

FABRICS (KNITS)

Fake fur fabrics and trims – these are synthetic fabrics that are also usually constructed on a knit base to give the feeling of real fur. High-quality fake furs are indistinguishable from the real thing, lighter in weight and reasonably easy to sew. The one drawback is that cutting the material can cause the fur to be shed in large quantities, and continuous vacuuming is a necessity. Asthmatics, and those with a sensitive respiratory system or allergies to certain fibres, need to pay special heed to this warning.

"Do not iron the top surface of fur fabric. Keep the iron plate well away from the fibres and only iron the back of the fabric if it absolutely needs to be pressed or a fusible applied. Keep a sheet of paper between the fabric and your iron plate. Melted fur fabric is highly unsightly!"

FABRICS (NON-WOVENS)

Felt – the best type of felt to use for 'soft' accessories for dress purposes is a medium-weight dress felt where the difference in the appearance of both sides is minimal. Felt is incredibly easy to cut, style and sew – a sewing machine will go through it with ease – and does not necessarily need neatening or hemming when cut, since the fibres are compacted and will not fray (see Wool fabrics).

Felt has a rather 'handcraft' image, but with a little effort can be elevated to achieve spectacular results. It also makes a good base for applying trims or other fabrics, as it possesses a degree of natural stability (See chapter 12).

Leather – the ease of cutting and punching and the general stability of leather make it a good choice for finishing a number of accessories with buckles, or providing a surface for decoration, as in a belt. For the projects in this book I have used a relatively thick cowhide leather. Leather from a sheep or pig will not work, being too soft and pliable. The leather can be marked with fineliners or a pencil, and cut with fabric scissors, a scalpel or, for the leatherworkers amongst you, a clicking knife (the latter being extremely sharp). Don't worry too much about the direction of the grain when you cut out the leather pieces, as, given the thickness and size of the pieces, this will be mainly immaterial for the projects in this book. This isn't a book about leathercraft, and the constraints of the project don't demand that the edges of a simple buckle strap need to be finished in any particular way; all that matters is that the pieces are cut as neatly and accurately as possible, using sharp scissors. Practice on scrap pieces of your chosen leather beforehand. Certain outlets will sell small pieces of leather of the right type and weight for buckles, which avoids having to buy a whole, comparatively expensive skin (see Stockists).

FABRICS (FUSIBLES)

Vilene® – this is the trade name for a group of fusibles available in a number of different weights and thicknesses. It is generally reckoned that a fusible material should be lighter in weight than the cloth it supports, though this need not always be the case. Generally, lighter-weight fabrics should partner with a lightweight but firm fusible material; heavier-weight fabrics with a heavier fusible.

I have a personal preference for Vilene® H 250 (lightweight but firm) and Vilene® H 640 (wadding material, suitable for quilting and very good in tandem with soft cottons). The ironing times and settings are printed on the side of the fabric.

Quiltex® – this is the trade name for Vilene® X50. The fabric has lines of glue which form a diagonal pattern and mark stitching lines when the fusible is ironed onto the main fabric. This enables diagonal quilting lines to be stitched accurately on whichever side of the fabric is more suitable (see chapter 13).

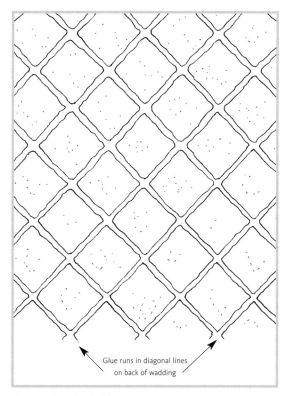

Glue runs in diagonal lines on back of wadding

The back of Quiltex® fabric.

tools

Scissors, hammer and punch.

Dressmaking scissors -- these should be used for cutting fabrics only, never paper, as this can blunt the blades. Good fabric scissors should be able to cut a wide range of materials, including leather of a medium thickness. Check the sharpness of your scissors on a regular basis.

Paper scissors – these will be invaluable for pattern-making. I recommend good all-purpose scissors as opposed to tiny paper scissors, since they save time when cutting out and are easier on the hands.

Pinking shears – can be used to provide a decorative finish to the fabric edges (see chapter 3).

Small curved manicure scissors – these actually work better than straight scissors for trimming threads and performing a variety of tasks.

Hammer – an ordinary tack hammer can be useful for fixing hardware such as eyelets and snap fasteners.

Steel block – of the type used in jewellery, this can provide a

good base when inserting eyelets, although is not strictly necessary for you to purchase as eyelet kits usually include a hammering base. I would recommend borrowing one if you can.

Pliers or wire cutters – these, and not scissors, should be used when cutting millinery wire.

Revolving fabric punch – this is capable of making holes of various sizes. I use this mainly for punching holes in leather buckles (although a standard punch which comes as part of an eyelet kit can be used just as effectively).

HANDSEWING EQUIPMENT

I'm assuming you already have a sewing kit, but here are some additional suggestions:

T-shaped pins – it is well worth investing in a box of T-shaped pins as opposed to dressmaking pins. These are useful for a number of projects, including millinery, and do not easily 'disappear'. A large box is expensive but well worth the investment. They are thicker than ordinary pins. I do not find that this affects the result, but would advise you to take care when using fine fabrics.

General sewing needles – I use quilting needles as these are short and slender and thus easier to do fine work with. I recommend a standard packet of size 5/10 needles, which will stand you in good stead for a number of projects.

Otherwise, a needle set incorporating a number of needles of about 3.8 cm (1¹/₂ in.), with a square head and small-to-medium-sized eye, will be ideal. This type of needle is very easy to manipulate and handle.

Beading needles – these will be necessary for items involving bead embroidery, since the head of conventional sewing needles is far too thick to go through the centre of most beads.

THREADS

Invisible sewing threads – these are made of nylon and are good for sewing some fine fabrics where a visible seam is undesirable. You may need to use a magnifier when working with them, as they are notoriously difficult to see! They also have a mind of their own and may loop around other parts of the item you are working on; take extra care that this does not happen when you are working.

Silk threads – these are suitable for projects involving silk fabrics, since cotton or cotton polyester will 'pull' the fabric too much. Where an item is made with a silk fabric I also try to tack it with a silk thread. This may seem rather wasteful, but conventional cotton polyester or polyester sewing thread has much thicker and harsher fibres than silk and can leave marks in the silk when the tacking threads are removed. Thus, silk thread is also useful for tacking lining fabrics which may mark easily (whatever the fibre content). Handle

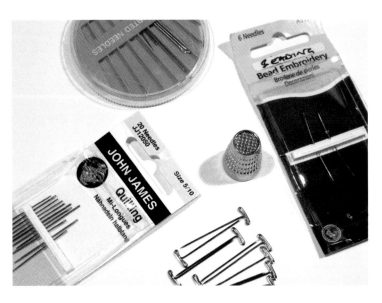

left: Pins and needles.
above: Invisible, polyester, silk and top-stitching threads.

fine and satin-weave fabrics more gently than you would fabrics of a superior weight and durability.

Polyester or cotton-polyester sewing threads – these are available in a wide range of colours and are highly suitable for most projects. Topstitching thread is a thicker variant of ordinary sewing thread and should be used for decorative topstitching only. When topstitching, the bobbin should be threaded with ordinary sewing thread.

Tape measure – ideally, this should be marked in both inches and cm, but either will do. The tape measure I have used throughout this book is marked in inches; I give alternative metric measurements alongside imperial measurements.

GLUES AND ADHESIVE TAPES

Nail glue or superglue – this is good for bonding items such as rhinestones to surfaces such as leather. I don't personally find hot-fix applicators that are available to fix rhinestones very effective, as the glue is not strong enough. Superglue generally only really works well on surfaces that aren't fibrous.

Nail glue.

❝NB Care must be taken when handling superglue, as skin and eyes can be easily bonded within seconds. If it does splash on skin, follow the manufacturer's advice for removal, or sand the area gently when dry with fine sandpaper. Do not attempt to peel glue away from skin, as the glue layer will invariably take several layers of skin with it. ❞

With the exception of certain millinery items and items that are made from materials other than soft fabrics, glues should not be used as a substitute for stitching. Firstly, they will not provide an adequate bond. Secondly, an item that is meant to move with the body should have flexibility, and should be designed with that in mind.

Adhesive tapes – these are useful for attaching pattern pieces to one another in the design stage to check fit, or for making a larger sheet of paper out of two smaller pieces. Easiest to work with, because of its matt top surface, is invisible tape; Sellotape® gives the best adhesion.

PAPER AND DRAWING EQUIPMENT, FABRIC MARKERS

Layout paper – this is great for planning and sketching designs and making patterns since it is semi-transparent. Buy a larger (A3) size since this offers more flexibility when designing larger items. If for any reason you run out of paper when making a pattern, tape two sheets of paper together using Sellotape®.

Tracing paper – this can be used for making mirrored designs, although layout paper, because of its transparency, can be just as effective. An A4 size block is usually adequate.

Thin art card – for making master patterns (that paper patterns can be made from).

Drafting pens, pencil, layout paper.

Propelling pencil – use for sketching designs and pattern drafting. This type of pencil can also be used to mark leather.

Fineliner pens – I buy packets of these in 0.1, 0.3, 0.5 and 0.7 mm sizes. They are good for making final patterns and also for marking leather.

Biro – surprisingly, I also use the humble biro for transferring patterns on occasion. I find the amount and quality of pressure exerted by the pen tip is able to transfer design from a chalked tracing very successfully to leather.

Draughtsman's eraser or putty rubber – for erasing, I prefer a draughtsman's rubber over a putty rubber, as putty rubbers leave a thin film of oil on the drawing surface, which attracts dirt.

Rulers and set squares – large rulers, approx. 45 cm (17³/₄ in.) long, and set squares are invaluable for pattern-making.

Compasses, protractor, French curves, rulers, set squares, circle template.

Protractors, compasses and French curves – protractors will help you measure angles accurately; compasses and French curves will enable you to create good, smooth curves within a pattern. I also use the following as fabric markers:

Tailor's chalk – available in several different colours but mainly white; good for transferring designs.

White pencil – this is good for marking dark-coloured fabrics. It does not need to be a specific fabric marker but can be an ordinary artist's white pencil; some softness of the lead is desirable in order to allow the design to be transferred easily. Marking fabric is not always necessary; in some instances pinning the pattern to the fabric is all that is needed prior to cutting out. However, fabric markers can be useful in instances where the fabric is very bulky or stretchy, and would be distorted if it were simply pinned to the pattern and cut out.

NOTIONS, FASTENINGS AND MISCELLANEOUS ITEMS

These include feathers (trim bought by the metre), tassels (bought as a trim or singly, usually for furnishing use), beads, rhinestones and found materials, toggles and fastenings. Depending on the type of product, both retailers and wholesalers will sell a minimum quantity of these items, or sell them packeted, rather than individually, since the unit price decreases when the item is bought in bulk. When buying materials of this type, it is a good idea to have a number of projects in mind for which they could be used.

Feathers – trims are usually bought by the metre or yard, with the feathers sewn into a band, and need to be considered a luxury. The least expensive tend to be undyed iridescent cock feathers. When using a sew-on feathered trim, the trim edge will need to be concealed in some way, either hidden in a seam or covered with an additional trim.

Ribbons – there are a wide variety of decorative ribbons on the market. Satin ribbons are available either double-faced or as a binding, in which case the edges are folded over towards the back. Most are synthetic, but the ribbon used in this book is bias-cut silk which is joined at intervals.

Leather trims are also joined diagonally in this way and, because of the consistency of leather necessary to make a good-quality leather trim, are very expensive. Organza ribbons are semi-transparent and have a slightly sparkly sheen; they mix well with applied bead embroidery. Ethnic bead trims

Left to right: trim, silk-ribbon binding, double-faced satin ribbon.

give that extra touch of authenticity to an accessory and can be bought at specialist outlets.

Petersham – normally used for millinery, it is also used to edge the collar in chapter 12. Buy curved, not straight, petersham, as this can be pulled into shape as you sew, to curve around the edge of the collar. The warmth of your hands will aid in pulling it into position, or you can also steam it into shape using an iron.

Elastic – a length of strong, wide elastic is useful for making belt sections. It aids in holding the belt around the waist, whilst simultaneously allowing for 'give' and movements of the body such as breathing in and out (see chapter 9).

Beads – these can be bought as a trim, or singly, or in colour-coordinated packets. When applied singly and by hand (as opposed to a sew-on trim which can be applied by machine), a beading needle should be used, as this has a thin head which will pass much more easily through the centre of small seed beads.

Rhinestones – these may be sew-on, or hot-fix stones (applied using a heated applicator), or simply need to be glued. I prefer not to 'hot-fix', being more in favour of superglue. Swarovski® rhinestones come in a variety of colours, styles and shapes including round, teardrop, leaf and square shapes. Patterns that successfully combine all these elements are well worth the effort to create (see chapter 9).

Leather thongs – these make useful ties for belts, are available in a variety of colours and can be purchased from bead suppliers.

Beads, trims and rhinestones.

Shells – I use cowrie shells for the Cowrie Belt described in chapter 7. They can be obtained relatively cheaply by mail order, but you may need to order a compulsory minimum quantity. Cowrie shells are very heavy when used in large numbers but add a touch of the exotic to an item.

Eyelets and snap fasteners – these are supplied in packs and should come with their own tools and instructions enclosed; these will vary according to the manufacturer. It is a good idea, if unfamiliar with the technique, to buy more of this type of product than you need, and to check carefully whether it is suitable for your chosen material and pattern.

Cover buttons – sold in sets; these are useful when a fastening harmonizing with the self-fabric is needed. A circle of fabric is cut, its edge tacked and pulled round the button, and the button base snapped on.

Hooks and eyes – these are good for fastening collars and other accessories. I recommend getting a large size of hook and eye (the fabric-covered type), rather than the smaller types bought on a card; the smaller types are not strong enough, have a tendency to unfasten themselves and will not hold the accessory in place.

Toggles – these come in two pieces (see chapter 12) and in various decorative finishes. They present an alternative method of fastening to a hook and eye, which may on occasion be stronger.

Buckles – a generic selection is generally available. It is essential that the buckle strap be compatible with the buckle itself. The buckle strap should be neither too narrow nor too wide, but able to be comfortably done, undone and pulled through. The design should take account of this.

OTHER MATERIALS

Wire – millinery wire is used for wiring the collar in chapter 12; this type of wire is available in several different thicknesses. The wire is paper- or thread-wrapped to increase its grip, and provides a highly stable support for projects that require a more defined or gravity-defying shape; the resulting shape will be simultaneously rigid but flexible. It should be cut with wire cutters; never use scissors as it will ruin their blades.

left: Eyelets, snap fasteners and cover buttons.
above: Miniature wire cutters and millinery wire.

SEWING MACHINE

Any machine will be suitable for the projects in this book, assuming that it is at least able to stitch through several layers of denim fabric, and two layers of 0.15 cm ($^1/_{16}$ in.) thickness cowhide leather.

Straight and zigzag stitches are necessary, as is a plentiful supply of sewing-machine needles for ordinary, leather and fine fabrics; expect to go through your needle supplies fast, depending on your usage of your machine. You will also need a zipper foot. I find this incredibly useful for all kinds of things, not just to insert zips, but to edge buckles or topstitch the edges of items made from bulky fabrics, stitch down fastenings, apply bindings or appliqué, or use piping cord.

A roller foot may be suitable for fabrics, such as plastics or certain ribbons, that are difficult to push through the machine using an ordinary foot. I also use a quilting attachment to create the equidistantly spaced quilting in chapter 8. This can be set to a particular width and used to space the sewing lines. It is part of my sewing-machine equipment; check your machine specifications to see whether such an item is available for your machine. If not, I give instructions for making the item in an alternative way.

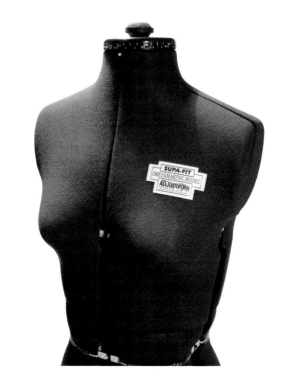

Tailor's dummy.

DRESSMAKING MODELS

A tailor's dummy that can be adjusted to the requisite measurements aids the designing and fitting process considerably. Though there is of course no substitute for fitting on the actual wearer, the dummy enables necessary adjustments to be more easily seen and made.

SEWING TECHNIQUES

The articles in this book are produced using a mixture of both hand- and machine-sewing. Either technique can be substituted for the other when practicalities preclude the use of one technique.

Handsewing is used in this book to sew delicate fabrics (such as the ribbon bindings in chapter 5), to attach fragile braids or trims, to embroider, or to make a neat finish. I use a variant of oversewing or hemstitching. To catch fabric in an area, I make what I call a few 'catch' stitches (several small stitches in one spot) to secure the fabric at that point. Hand embroidery with beads is used for two projects (see chapters 7 and 12). Machine-stitching I use where hand-stitching would be inadvisable, usually where it is necessary to stitch through several layers of fabric.

3 felt boa

Get scissor-happy with the pinking shears; this dramatic boa made from layers of shocking pink and black felt is given an almost organic touch with serrated, fringed edges, and is very easy to make. There is no handsewing needed. Three 15 cm (6 in.) x 177 cm (70 in.) layers of felt are sandwiched together, machine-stitched down their central length and then cut into a fringe at both sides; this is the part that actually takes the time, but which makes the creation of this fun-looking, voluminous and warm piece all the more worthwhile.

I don't provide a pattern for this design, as you can actually measure and work directly on the felt, but if you are unsure about the quantities you are pur-chasing, it may well be a good idea to make a basic pattern for the felt strips, which are all the same dimensions.

This piece was made from good wool dress felts of a generous width. Purchase these if you can, since the longer the pieces you can cut, the longer, and thus more dra-matic, your boa will be! Depending on the purchased quantity, you may also be able to make several boas from the same length of fabric. Choose a good-quality medium-weight dress felt which shows a minimal difference in the visual appearance between each side (some thicker or more heavy-weight felts have a definite 'wrong' side), and which is relatively thin and not too obviously fibrous.

step-by-step method

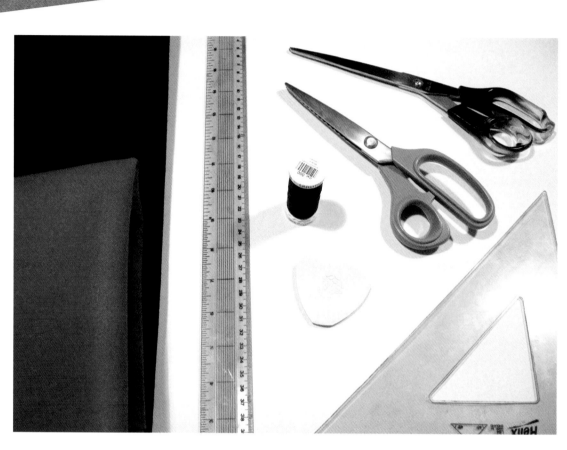

Materials you will need: pink and black felt, tailor's chalk, sewing thread, pinking shears, fabric scissors, set square.

YOU WILL NEED

- ▸ Pink dress felt
- ▸ Black dress felt
- ▸ Tailor's chalk (or white pencil)
- ▸ Sewing thread (matching)

- ▸ Pins
- ▸ Fabric scissors
- ▸ Pinking shears
- ▸ Set square

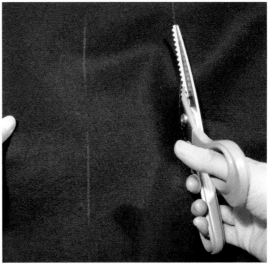

Using the tailor's chalk and set square, mark out two 15 cm (6 in.) by 177 cm (70 in.) pieces of pink felt and one piece of the same dimensions in black felt. Mark the longitudinal centre (running from end to end) of the pieces with a chalked dashed line.

Cut the pieces of felt using pinking shears.

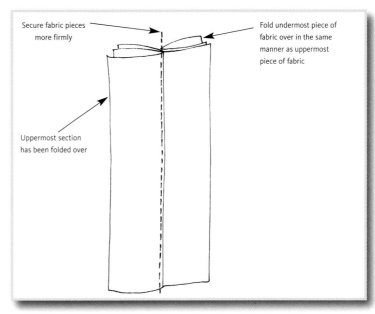

Secure fabric pieces more firmly

Fold undermost piece of fabric over in the same manner as uppermost piece of fabric

Uppermost section has been folded over

Pin the pieces of felt together in a sandwich so that the pieces of pink felt are on top, and stitch down the middle (see illustration). Then, fold over one of the layers of felt and stitch along the fold to make a seam that follows the line of, and falls on top of, the previous seam you made. This secures the fabric pieces more firmly and gives added body to the scarf.

Cut a fringe along all free edges of the fabric using conventional dressmaking scissors – it is easiest to cut perhaps two layers at a time, as evenness of cutting will be distorted if additional layers are cut at this point. The fringe sections do not need to be perfectly straight; they can be cut at slightly acute angles that veer gradually towards the vertical and back again.

Using pinking shears, chop into the fringe – this is the most arduous and time-consuming part. If possible, protect your hands with a layer of cloth wrapped around the handles of your scissors, or take breaks in between cutting sections.

SCARVES, COLLARS, TIES & BELTS

The finished boa.

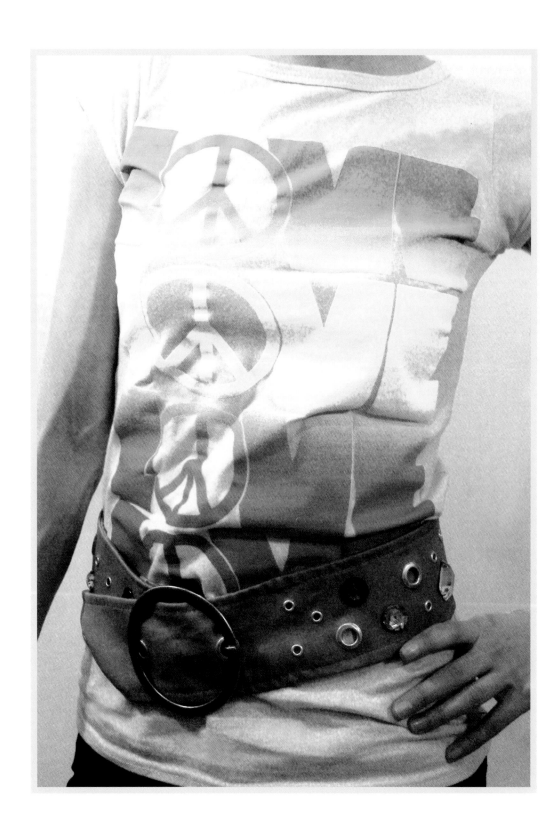

4 eyelet belt

This long, wide belt is made of medium to lightweight turquoise denim, decorated with eyelets and sew-on jewels of varying sizes, and finished with a large 7.5 cm (3 in.) buckle. Designed to fit most sizes, it can be worn at the waist or hip level, any excess in the belt length being allowed to hang free or being tucked into the jewelled section.

No additional fusible stiffening or support fabric will be needed to make the belt, as the double layer of denim will already have sufficient stability when the belt is seamed and topstitched. The seaming lends extra shape and definition to the denim, which is readily manipulated. Using stiffen-ing fabric is also likely to make your work harder when it comes to inserting eyelets, as you will have to pierce holes for each eyelet through several layers of fabric.

If you have never worked with eyelets before, I suggest buying more eyelet kits than you need and practising beforehand to familiarise yourself with the technique, as a certain amount of wastage can occur with inexperience. Most eyelet kits come with their own tools, which may be ready for use or may need to be assembled. It is important to hammer into the dead centre of the eyelet tool, because if it is done off-centre the eye-let will squash to one side and eventually work loose.

step-by-step method

Some materials you will need: denim, large buckle, scissors, hammer, tape measure, eyelets of varying sizes, sew-on rhinestones.

YOU WILL NEED

▶ Denim (light to medium weight)

▶ Large 7.5 cm (3 in.) buckle

▶ Polyester sewing thread (matching)

▶ Needle

▶ Tape measure

▶ Fabric scissors

▶ White pencil for fabric marking

▶ Hammer

▶ Large sew-on jewels or rhinestones

▶ Sets of eyelets of varying sizes – 11 mm (7/16 in.) and 4 mm (3/16 in.) recommended

For pattern see page 132.

Pin and tack the belt pattern to the denim before cutting out.

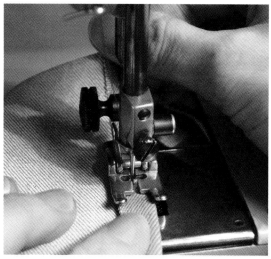

Fold under and stitch across the short, straight ends of each belt piece to neaten them.

Placing the belt pieces WS to WS, stitch up the sides of the belt, working from the pointed end to the squared-off ends.

Turn the belt inside out and press.

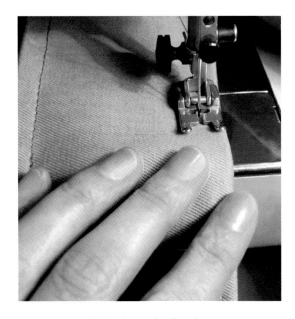

Topstitch the belt edge on both sides.

Fold under the edges of the squared-off end of the belt, pinning or tacking if need be, and topstitch.

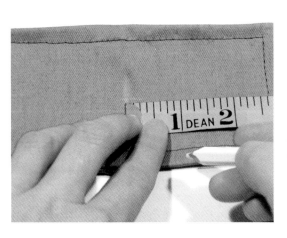

Mark the position for an eyelet at the straight end of the belt with a cross, both in the centre of the belt and 7.5 cm (3 in.) from the end. This will be the point at which the buckle is fastened.

Insert a large eyelet at the marked position, and check its fit with the buckle.

The reverse of the belt.

Fold the end of the belt under, then topstitch through all layers to hold the buckle in position.

Mark positions for large eyelets placed 7.5 cm (3 in.) apart towards the opposite end of the belt, for fastening (fit the belt to the wearer beforehand to check appropriate positions).

Insert large eyelets at the marked positions.

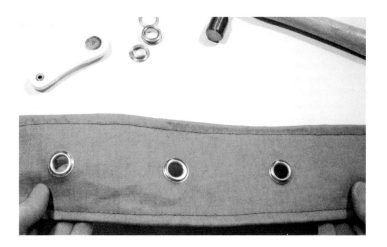

Between the eyelets at each end of the belt, arrange sew-on rhinestones and eyelets of different sizes randomly so that they give a pleasing effect. Mark their positions carefully, using a white pencil and different symbols, before attaching them; take a photographic record if necessary. Insert the eyelets prior to attaching the rhinestones, as a stray blow from the hammer used to fix the eyelets may damage the rhinestones.

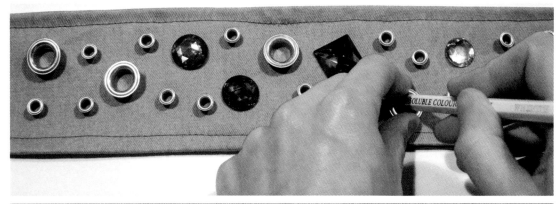

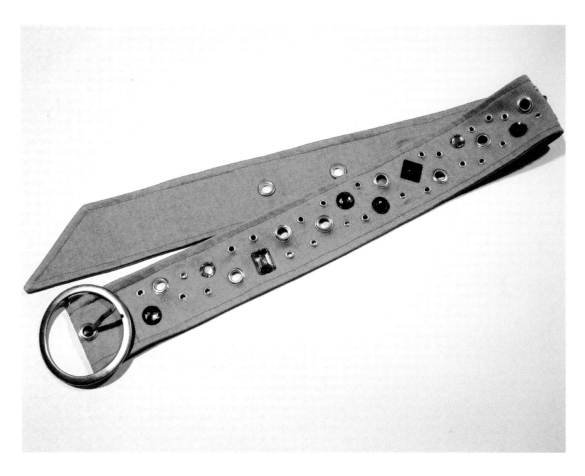

The finished belt.

5 folded ribbon tie-belt

We delve into the realms of fabric manipulation here; this ribbon tie-belt is made using a beautiful floral-patterned silk bias-cut ribbon, with attached panels of folded ribbon in a repeated pattern along its length. Easy to make, using only handstitching and no machine-stitching, the tie can be worn either at the neck, with a corsage attached, or at the waist, as the finishing touch for a summer dress.

step-by-step method

Materials: ribbon binding, fabric scissors, invisible thread, tape measure, needles.

YOU WILL NEED

▶ 8 m (9 yd) of 2.5 cm (1 in.) single-sided silk-ribbon binding
▶ Invisible thread
▶ Tacking thread (silk)

▶ Needle
▶ Tape measure
▶ Fabric scissors

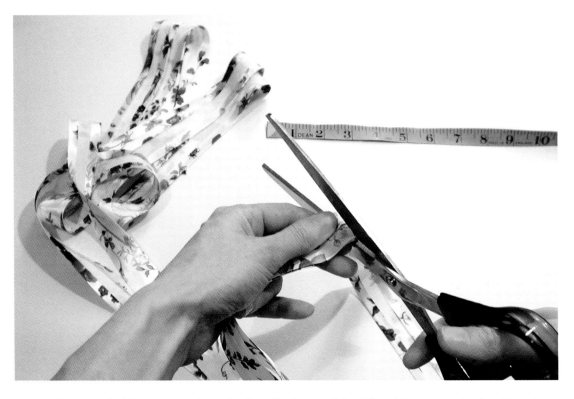

Cut two lengths of ribbon binding from the 8 m (9 yd) strip 1$^1/_2$ m (60 in.) long, to make the ribbon base for the belt.

Tack the two strips of ribbon together gently using silk tacking thread and a diagonal tacking stitch (this holds better than a stitch applied horizontally or vertically to the length of ribbon).

Cut about 2.5 cm (1 in.) of ribbon off the ends, to neaten.

Fold over each end of the double ribbon strip and tack down.

Using invisible thread, oversew the long edges of the double ribbon strip together. Make sure the stitches are small, neat and evenly spaced. Do not pull the thread too tightly, but make sure it does not catch around anything else and create a loop which will be visible later (one of the pleasures of working with invisible thread!).

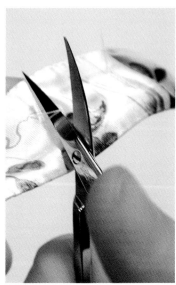

Remove the tacking stitches carefully.

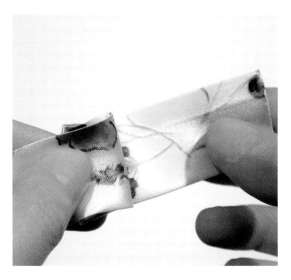

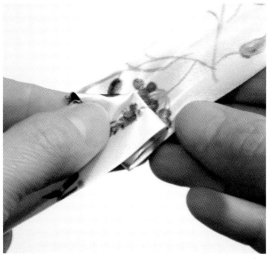

Cut four 1m (40 in.) pieces from the original long length of ribbon. Take one of these and fold the end back on itself a short distance, then back again to make a small concertina fold.

Fold each corner of the fold inwards to give a triangular shape reminiscent of a paper hat. This folded unit will be repeated along the ribbon lengths, and held in place with short stitches.

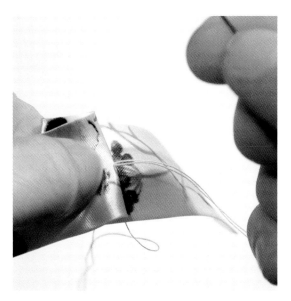

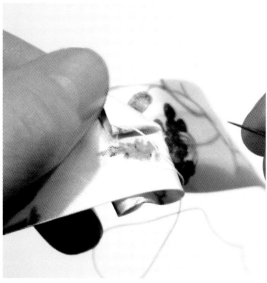

Tacking down the first concertina fold.

Tacking down the triangular part of the fold.

Continue the process until eight units have been tacked into position. Using the remaining three 1 m (40 in.) lengths, make four of these eight-unit pieces in all; these will be sewn to the longer ribbon strip to decorate it.

Trim the folded piece 5 cm (2 in.) from the first triangular-folded unit.

Now secure the folded units permanently with invisible thread. Stitch the centre of the fold first.

Stitch the triangular part into position by sewing the underside of the fold to the layer beneath. Do not stitch through the top layer. This will give your folds a pleasing 'bounce' and three-dimensional shape, rather than being just stitched down flat.

Remove the tacking threads.

Trim the very end of the folded piece 2.5 cm (1 in.) from the final folded unit.

Position the folded ribbon piece so that it covers one end of the long ribbon length.

Pin and tack the folded ribbon piece to the double ribbon length, tucking the ends of both pieces underneath.

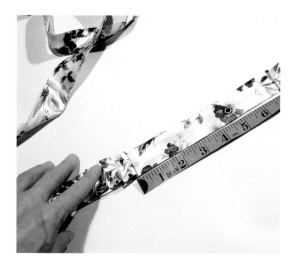

Measure 17.5 cm (7 in.) from the end of the folded ribbon section. Position one end of a second folded ribbon piece at this point so that it extends further up the tie, and so that the triangular folded sections point towards those of the first section.

Using invisible thread, stitch the folded ribbon pieces to the belt base by catching just the top of the first triangle's fold. Pass the needle through the back of the ribbon piece to the front, before inserting it into the underlying ribbon-tie base and running it through the space between the two layers of ribbon. Bring the needle up through the next fold and repeat as before. This will, again, prevent the ribbon folds from appearing as though they have been stitched down 'flat'.

Secure the short edges of the ribbon pieces using oversewing at their ends, and hemstitching further up the belt base.

Remove the tacking.

The finished belt.

6 pompom scarf

Give designer gear a run for its money with this fun 'city' scarf made from good-quality, soft-wool tweed-inspired fabric, and pompoms made from lengths of fake-fur garment edging. Additional features include large tucks to give a strong, positive shape to the neck, and a black-leather neck strap with buckles to give support, and a 'designer' touch, to this area.

Caution should be exercised when cutting the fake fur for the pompoms: the fur goes everywhere, and, short of cutting the fabric out on a sticky surface, there is little that can be done to remedy this except rigorous and continuous vacuuming. Asthmatics, as well as those with a sensitive respiratory system or who have allergies to certain fibres, may need to take care, as the fibres become airborne and can be inhaled. The photographs you see in this chapter omit the 'after cutting' stage for a good reason! Wear a basic protective mask for this process if it concerns you.

The medium weight wool fabric I chose for the scarf needed no additional stiffening fabric to help it keep its shape; the wadding on the materials list overleaf is used for stuffing the pompoms. The buckle strap is made of leather; this can be cut with sharp fabric scissors, and I don't advocate any special finishes other than that the leather should be cut with care, neatly and symmetrically. You will also need brushes and Copydex® glue to attach the leather pieces to each other prior to stitching, since you will be unable to tack them in position.

step-by-step method

Materials needed: black fur trim (or fur fabric), preferably soft, good-quality wool fabric suiting; Copydex® glue, tacking thread, sewing thread, revolving punch, pencil, old brush, fabric scissors, needle, buckles, wadding, leather pieces, tape measure.

YOU WILL NEED

- ▸ Fake-fur fabric or fake-fur trim – 10 cm (4 in.) fake-fur trim used in this example
- ▸ Wool fabric
- ▸ Leather pieces
- ▸ Wadding (Vilene® H640)
- ▸ Matching polyester thread

- ▸ Tacking thread
- ▸ Needle
- ▸ Pins
- ▸ Tape measure
- ▸ Ordinary drawing pencil (soft)
- ▸ Fabric scissors

- ▸ Revolving fabric punch
- ▸ 2 x 1.6 cm (5/8 in.) wide buckles
- ▸ Copydex® glue
- ▸ Old brush
- ▸ Sewing machine with zipper foot

For pattern see page 133.

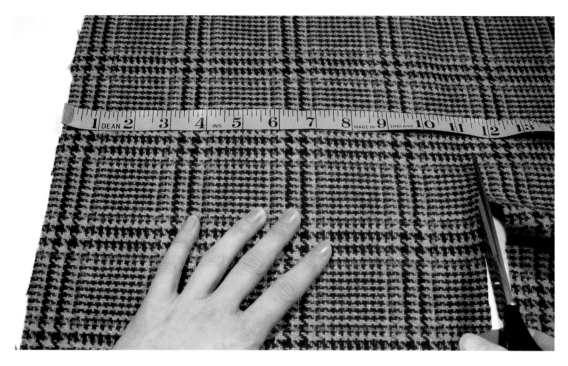

Cut a rectangular piece of the wool fabric, 28 cm (11 in.) wide and 163 cm (64 in.) long.

Drawing round your pattern using pencil, transfer the leather neck-support and buckle-strap shapes onto the leather.

The pencil-drawn shapes should be just visible on the surface of the leather. On the neck support, mark in the points of buckle attachment and the midpoint that marks the centre back (CB).

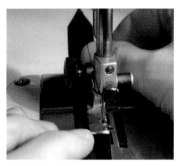

Using the zipper foot, stitch all round the edges of the buckle straps and neck support.

Cut out the neck support and the buckle-strap shapes. Punch holes using the revolving punch that corresponds to, or is suitable for, the size of your buckle.

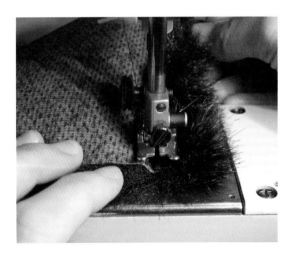

If using fake-fur trim as the fabric for your pom-poms, stitch two sections of trim together at their long edges. This will create an area of fabric large enough to cut the pompom shapes from.

Fold the wool fabric to make a long strip, RS (right side) to RS, and make a 0.6 cm (¼ in.) seam along the long edge.

Apply Copydex® to the last 2.5 cm (1 in.) of each buckle strap, placing these at each end of the neck support in line with the pencil marks.

Cut circles from the fake-fur trim or your chosen fake-fur fabric using the pompom pattern. (NB This is an untidy business, as the fibres from fake fur fabric go everywhere when the fabric is cut. Make sure that you work on a piece of white paper, and vacuum continuously. The picture shows a post-vacuuming scenario!)

Tack all round the edges of the fake-fur circles, about 0.6 cm ($^1/_4$ in.) from the edge and using a double thread so that the edge can be gathered.

Stuff the fake-fur circles with wadding fabric that has been torn up or folded down to a small size, then pull the threads tight and secure the resulting pompom with a couple of firm knots.

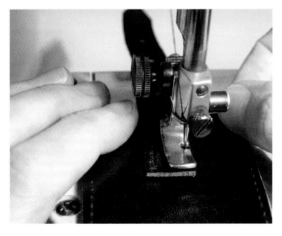

Using the topstitching of the buckle strap as a guideline, stitch the buckle strap to the neck support using a zipper foot.

Topstitch 1.27 cm ($^{1}/_{2}$ in.) in from the seamed (not folded) long edge of the scarf to give it shape and prevent it from 'collapsing'.

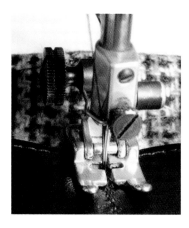

Find the CB of the scarf by folding it in half widthways. Place the neck support on top of the scarf, aligning the CB points. Stitch down the middle of the neck support, through all fabric layers, to secure it in position.

Insert the ends of the scarf into the pompoms and secure well with several handstitches.

Measure 7.5 cm (3 in.) and 15 cm (6 in.) from the edge of the neck support. Mark these positions with pins.

Make tucks on either side of the neck support at the points marked with pins. The direction of the tucks should be mirrored on both sides, with the tucks facing towards the CB.

Machine-stitch backwards and forwards over the midpoints of the tucks several times using a matching thread.

Handstitch the centre bar of a buckle at a point just past the last tuck on either side.

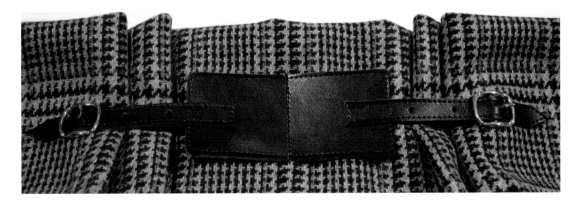

Fasten the buckle straps.

The finished scarf.

7 cowrie belt

Different colours of bias-cut, machined, patchwork strips of Benares brocade combine with multicoloured glass beads, cowrie shells and leather thongs to tie this ethnic-look belt, which incidentally works just as well styled round the neck as a semi-collar or jewellery item. Perfect for sunshine holidays or summer nights in the tropics!

Benares brocade is available in many different colours. Typically, the fabric is a silk and viscose brocade of a single colour with a gold or silver-coloured metallic pattern; the metal content is high. It is advisable to iron with a sheet of paper between the iron plate and the fabric, and not to iron using too hot a setting. The brocade threads can also pull easily, so care is needed when working with the fabric. The pieces that make up the belt are deliberately bias-cut in order to create a pleasing line when the item wraps around the body. If they were cut on a straight grain and seamed as vertical sections there would be less strength in the resulting fabric as any pull on the belt would be at right angles to the seam, creating a strain on this delicate material. A diagonal seam avoids this, and also looks more attractive.

When purchasing cowries, buy a good-sized bag, as some may need to be rejected since piercing is not always accurate, thus making it impossible to draw a needle and thread through the two holes in the back of the shell.

The belt is made from a very simple strip pattern; cowrie shells are attached to the front in groups of three, where their orientation is horizontal, and along the main section (which marks the back) in a single line, where their orientation is also horizontal. They are complemented by multicoloured loops of glass beads that create a slightly 'wavy' pattern when worked en masse.

The belt pattern is also used to make the pattern for the stiffener; the main belt pattern is simply drawn onto the stiffener and the shape trimmed by 0.3 cm ($1/8$ in.) from the drawn edge all the way round.

step-by-step method

Materials you may need: pieces of Benares brocade, firm fusible stiffener, cowries, set square, multicoloured beads, white pencil, fineliner, leather thong, fabric scissors, matching thread, beading needle.

YOU WILL NEED

- Benares brocade in several different colours
- Vilene® H250
- Leather thong, 3 m (4 yd)
- Matching thread

- Tacking thread
- Needle
- Beading needle
- White pencil
- Fineliner

- Multicoloured opaque-glass seed beads
- Fabric scissors
- Set square

For pattern see page 134.

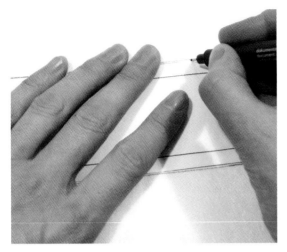

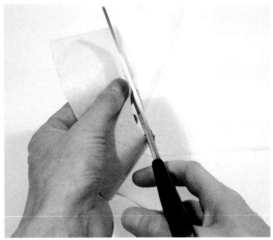

Draw around the main belt pattern onto the fusible stiffener with a fineliner.

Cut out the stiffener, 0.3 cm (⅛ in.) in from the marked edge.

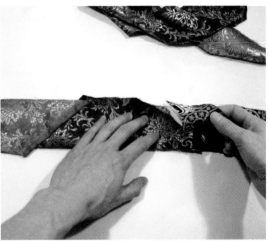

Mark the bias on the Benares brocade with a white pencil and set square.

Cut out several pieces of different-coloured Benares brocade on the bias, then arrange them to fit the shape of the belt pattern so that their diagonal edges can be fitted together. The diagonal edge gives a stronger and more pleasing finish than would straight joins.

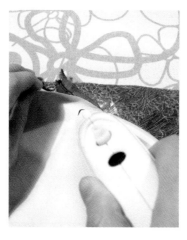

Stitch the brocade pieces RSS together.

Iron the seams flat, using a sheet of paper between the iron plate and fabric.

Pin the pattern to the pieces of brocade and cut round it (make two belt sections).

Iron the fusible stiffener onto one section of the brocade.

Tack the belt sections RSS together.

Stitch the belt sections together, leaving the entire pointed sections of each end open.

Turn the belt right side out and press, placing a sheet of paper underneath the iron plate to protect both it and the fabric.

Cut the length of leather thong in half and, doubling one of the halves, insert it into one of the open ends of the belt, securing it with tacking stitches.

Oversew the pointed ends of the belt together, turning the seams under as you go and making sure that the ends mirror each other and are symmetrical. Sew in between the two ends of the thong to secure it. Repeat this for the other end.

Topstitch 1cm ($^3/_8$ in.) from the edge of the belt to define its shape.

Using a beading needle and sewing thread, stitch cowries into place at the ends and middle of the belt; a conventional sewing needle may have too large an eye. Make at least two or three stitches through each cowrie to secure it; ensure that the thread is pulled fairly tight and does not become caught in or loop around anything.

Again, using a beading needle, stitch tiny glass beads to the belt. Thread 12 beads onto the thread, then attach them at a point approximately 1.5 cm (⅝ in.) from the starting point so that they form loops; several of these loops sewn close together will make a wavy pattern.

Pattern detail.

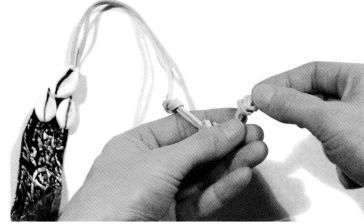

Make knots in the thongs in order to strengthen them and to add a decorative element.

The finished belt.

8 indian scarf

Using authentic Indian fabrics and trims together with wadding along its length, this quilted Indian scarf not only provides warmth but also an interesting, eye-catching and dramatic shape as it is styled around the neck. This is achieved through the bulk of the wadding combined with the double layer of cotton. Vintage Indian metallic and pompom trims are added to give a truly authentic feel.

Spend some time choosing fabrics and trims that work well together. I deliberately chose hot, spicy, contrasting colours because to me these best represented the spirit of India. The pompom trim is essential – this type of trim comes in a number of different bright colours, with red, pink and orange being more usual.

If the piece of antique trim you purchase is slightly dilapidated, with beads or wires missing, spend some time repairing it carefully, catching any stray threads and stitching them down, working with a neutral-coloured silk thread that blends with the ground colour of the trim. The foundation fabrics of the trim may well be of very delicate silk fabrics; take your time to ensure that no parts of the design can come loose.

step-by-step method

Materials needed: Indian cotton print fabric, wadding, silk threads to repair, sew-on trims, tape measure, needle, fabric scissors.

YOU WILL NEED

- Printed Indian cotton
- Wadding (Vilene® H640)
- Vintage Indian trim, 7.5–9 cm (3–3½ in.)wide and 30 cm (12 in.) long

- Vintage Indian pompom trim, 30 cm (12 in.) long
- Matching silk thread
- Contrasting silk thread (for tacking)
- Needle

- Pins
- Tape measure
- White pencil (optional)
- Fabric scissors
- Sewing machine with zipper foot

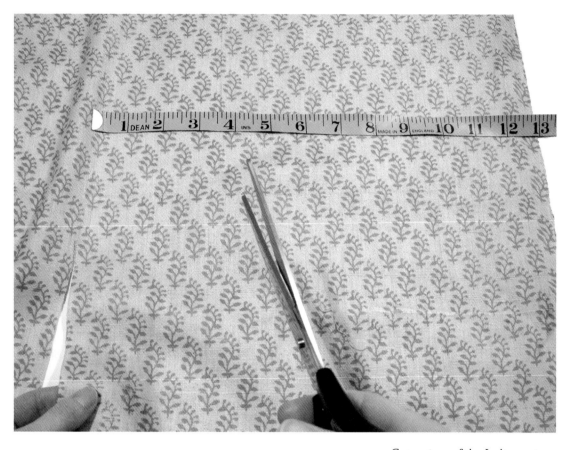

Cut a piece of the Indian cotton print fabric, 33 cm (13 in.) wide and 1.5 m (60 in.) long.

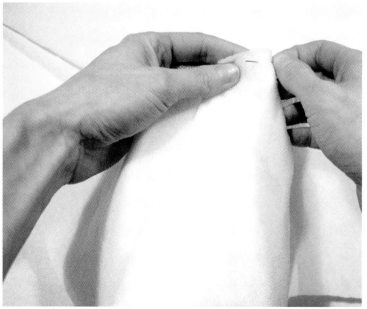

Cut wadding equal to half the width of the strip of print fabric. If the wadding is not long enough, join two strips together by lightly backstitching; this join, which may seem to create lumps and bumps to start with, will eventually be disguised by the quilting pattern and the thickness of the outer fabric.

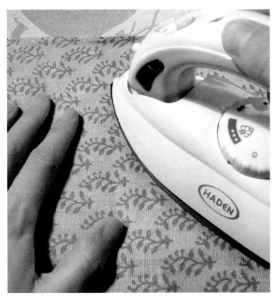

Iron the wadding onto one half of the fabric with the RS of the outer fabric face up, in order to avoid damage to the iron plate from the synthetic wadding, which is soft and fibrous on its non-adhesive side. Leave about 2.5 cm (1 in.) extra width along one side. This side will be turned under to neaten the scarf.

Fold the unwadded half of the scarf material over the wadding longitudinally (along its length), so that a sandwich of fabric and wadding is made. Pin the sandwich along its length and tack.

SCARVES, COLLARS, TIES & BELTS

Quilt the scarf along its length in rows, using lines of quilting spaced 2.5 cm (1 in.) apart. A quilting attachment makes things much quicker and easier. If you do not have a quilting attachment, you will need to pre-mark the quilting lines using a white pencil or equidistantly spaced tacking. Leave about 2.5 cm (1 in.) free at the edge.

Bring the long edges of the scarf together, then turn them under on one side of the scarf so that the wadding is completely enclosed. Pin and tack, then stitch just inside the turned-under edge to secure it using a zipper foot.

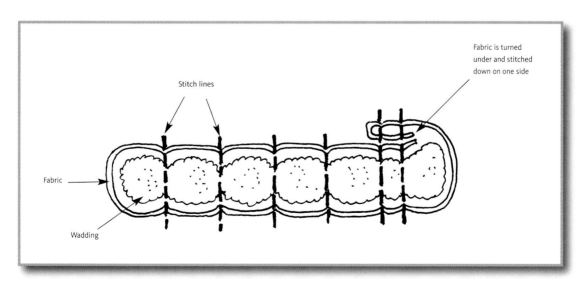

Cross section of the scarf.

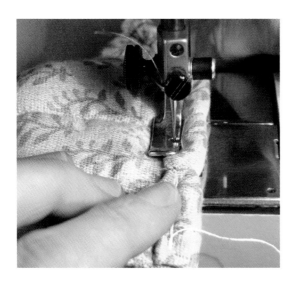

Turn under and tack each short end of the scarf. Stitch the ends with a zipper foot in the same way as you stitched the longer side.

Cut lengths of pompom braid to fit across each short end of the scarf. Tack and hemstitch both edges of each length of braid to the ends of the scarf.

Having repaired the embroidered trim where necessary, cut pieces to fit each short end of the scarf. Tack the pieces on gently above the pompom trim, using silk thread.

Stitch the edges of the embroidered trim to the scarf using hemstitching.

The finished scarf.

9 bollywood belt

This belt is made from leather pieces with a colourful Swarovski® rhinestone decoration. Rhinestones of different shapes and colours are mounted on a belt front of cowhide leather to form a sparkling, stylised paisley pattern. The belt is further accessorised and fastened with large silver snap fasteners that provide extra decorative interest as well as opening and closing the belt. It should be worn high, rather than low, on the waist, and also looks great worn with a crop top – perfect Bollywood-inspired style!

The belt is also partially elasticated. The belt front attaches to a section of wide elastic that forms the back of the belt. This section of elastic is cut to suit the wearer's waist size.

The rhinestones are carefully attached to the leather ground following a marked pattern in tailor's chalk and using superglue. I do not recommend electrical rhinestone applicators that claim to 'hot-fix' rhinestones. They are expensive, and generally the glue is not strong enough, meaning that the stones do not fix. Superglue is not infallible, but in my opinion is the best adhesive. It's always advisable to keep a few stones of each colour spare in case of loss.

The pattern on page 135 shows the belt pattern, together with an indication of the size and type of rhinestones needed. Experiment with different placements and quantities of the rhinestones to get a different interpretation of the pattern.

step-by-step method

Materials: Hammer, steel block (extra support when fixing snap fasteners), tracing paper, wide elastic, snap-fastener kit, nail glue and pins OR hot-fix rhinestone applicator, biro, tape measure, tailor's chalk, fabric scissors, white pencil, assortment of rhinestones, leather pieces.

YOU WILL NEED

▸ Pieces of cowhide leather (for belt front) 0.15 cm (¹⁄₁₆ in.) thick.

▸ Wide elastic 7.5 cm (3 in.) wide; length = waist measurement of wearer minus 20 cm (8 in.)

▸ Rhinestones (see pattern for types and quantities, or select your own)

▸ Biro

▸ Tailor's chalk

▸ White pencil

▸ Pins

▸ Tape measure

▸ Fabric scissors

▸ Tracing paper

▸ Nail glue

▸ Hot-fix rhinestone applicator (optional)

▸ Hammer

▸ Steel block (optional)

▸ Snap-fastener kit 15 mm (⁹⁄₁₆ in.)

▸ Sewing machine

For pattern see page 135.

Draw the belt pattern to scale and trace it using biro.

Chalk the back of the tracing with tailor's chalk.

Trace the pattern onto the leather using a biro; you'll find the pressure gives a better result than pencil.

Cut out the pattern pieces with fabric scissors, leaving about 0.6 cm (¼ in.) from the line.

Stitch inside the pattern line, making a line of stitching inside the edges and across the width of the belt to one side of the snap-fastener position on each side, as shown.

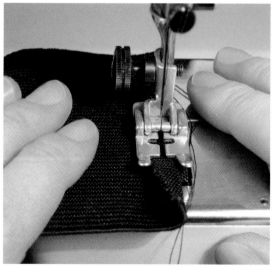

Cut the elastic to size; it should equal the wearer's waist measurement minus 23 cm (9 in.). Stitch each end of the elastic section across its width, turning the edge of the fabric under about 1 cm (³⁄8 in.) as you go, to neaten.

Trim the leather pieces all round to where they are marked, about 0.3 cm ($^1/_8$ in.) from the seams.

Punch holes in the leather using the punch from your snap-fastener kit. Then place a piece of leather over the end of the elastic and, using a white pencil, mark the snap-fastener positions using the punched leather as a template.

Fix the snap fasteners in position in the manner shown.

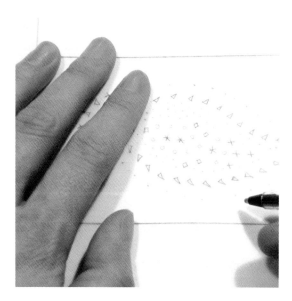

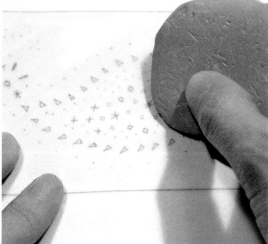

Trace the paisley design using a biro (the same tracing can be used for both sides of the belt, as they mirror each other).

Chalk the back of the tracing with tailor's chalk.

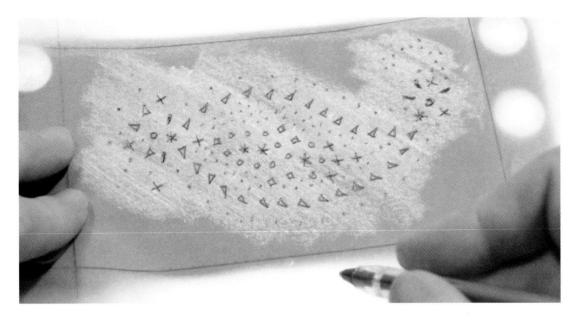

Place the chalked tracing over the belt section, aligning the straight outer edges of the design with the stitching just inside the horizontal edges of the belt front, and transfer the design to the belt section using a biro.

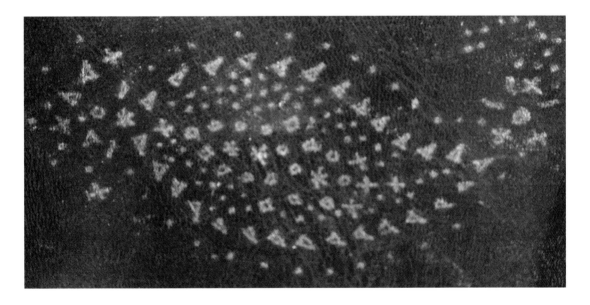

The transferred design.

You can try using a hot-fix tool to fix the appropriate hot-fix rhinestones (not all rhinestones are compatible with the tool).

I prefer to fix the rhinestones to the leather base in the following way: applying a bead of nail glue to a pin, then picking up a rhinestone with the pin before guiding it into position. The superglue is much stronger than 'hot-fix' glue.

Do the same for the opposite belt panel so that the two panels form mirror images of each other. Congratulations! Your belt is now finished!

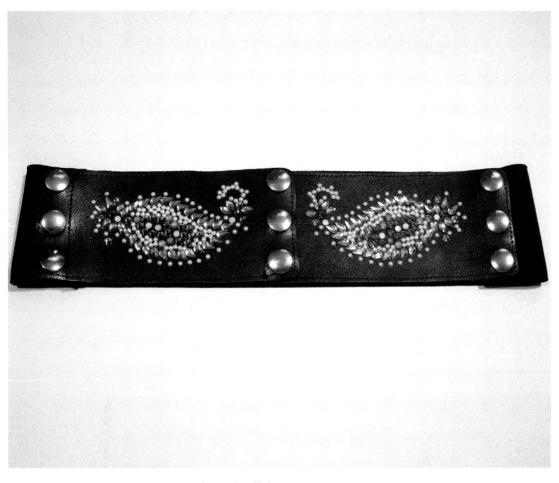

The completed belt.

10 polka dot collar

This very simple-to-make collar gives a classic, light and airy touch to a business suit, or other formal or semi-formal outfit. Made of semi-transparent, light polka-dot-print cotton polyester, it is formed from a tube of fabric drawn over a self-fabric-covered, lightly stiffened base. The tube is longer than the base, which means that volume and an almost ruched silhouette are created when the tube is drawn over the base and sewn in position. One side is then decorated with a self-fabric bow made out of another long tube of fabric, and the opposite side fastened with a covered button and loop. Note that although the fabric itself is light and airy, it has just enough bulk, when manipulated in the ways described below, to give the collar shape.

NB: this collar is made to fit a 33 cm (13 in.) neck. The finished collar will measure 40 cm (16 in.) in length. I recommend using the neck measurement of the wearer and adding 10 cm (4 in.) to the pattern length for ease. When making the fusible pattern to fit the collar, ensure that it is at least as long as the collar fabric base, and 6.3 cm (2½ in.) wide. The collar base itself is cut on the bias; the bow and covering fabric on the straight grain.

step-by-step method

You will need: polka-dot fabric, thin but firm stiffener, sewing thread, needle, cover button, fineliner, pencil, fabric scissors, set square, ruler.

YOU WILL NEED

- Lightweight polka-dot fabric (suggested: cotton polyester)
- Vilene® H250
- Matching cotton-polyester thread

- Tacking thread
- Needle
- Cover button, 19 mm (³⁄₄ in.)
- Fineliner

- Pencil
- Set square
- Ruler
- Fabric scissors

For pattern see page 136.

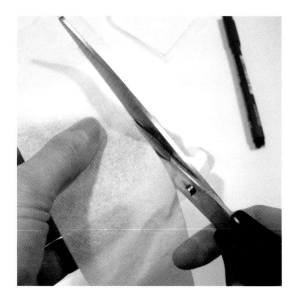

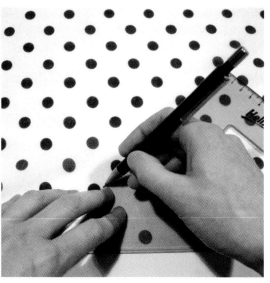

Trace around the main pattern onto the fusible stiffener with a fineliner, then trim off 0.6 cm (¼ in.) all the way round.

Draw a diagonal line on the polka-dot fabric to mark the bias using a set square.

Pin the pattern for the collar base to the fabric, aligned on the bias, and cut out.

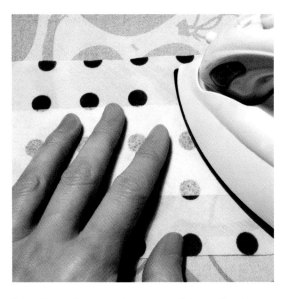

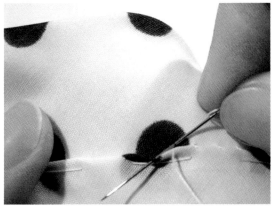

Iron the stiffener to the centre of the polka-dot fabric.

Fold the excess fabric at either side over the stiffened part of the collar base so that both pieces overlap. Fold the edge of the uppermost piece underneath and tack. Then stitch the edge to the underlying piece of fabric using a hemstitch and small imperceptible stitches.

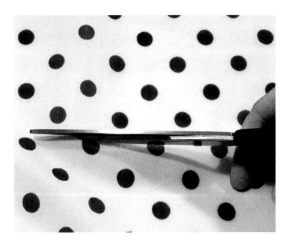

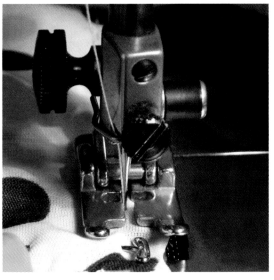

Cut out two pieces of fabric on the straight grain, 15 cm (6 in.) wide and 86 cm (34 in.) long; the polka-dot pattern can be used as a guideline.

Zigzag-stitch along the ends of the fabric pieces to neaten (see above), then fold the fabric pieces in half longitudinally and stitch them along their long sides to make two tubes.

Fold the ends of the collar support under, and stitch to secure.

Pull one of the fabric tubes onto the collar support so it gives an almost 'ruched' effect, and pin it at either end of the support to hold it in position.

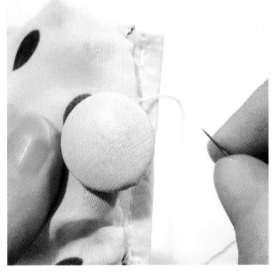

Turn the ends of the tube under just short of the ends of the support so that the collar-support seam is exposed; tack at this point to hold the fabric in position, and hemstitch the turned-under edge of the tube to the collar-support seam to secure it imperceptibly.

Make a cover button with self-fabric and sew it to the centre of one end of the collar.

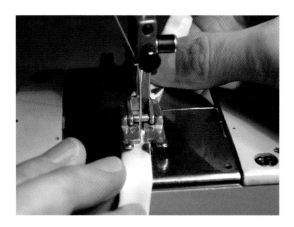

Cut a strip of fabric 2.5 cm (1 in.) wide and 10 cm (4 in.) long. Fold it in half along its length. Fold both long edges under so that the folds lie on top of each other, then topstitch the folded strip along its length.

Make a loop from the folded strip of fabric and stitch it in a position that corresponds to the button on the opposite side of the collar and ensures a good fit (check the fit before stitching in position).

Style a soft 'bow' from the other tube of fabric by looping it in a loose concertina fashion and tacking it onto the side of the collar in a position that diametrically opposes the button fastening.

Secure the bow with neat, imperceptible stitches to catch it in position.

The finished collar.

11 folded silk tie

This piece is a bit more complicated than some of the other pieces in the book, and probably more suitable for those with some experience. Made in a fabulous, intensely coloured lime-green heavyweight tie silk, its fabric is manipulated to create a pattern of fishtail folds down the tie. This is made possible by creating the tie in several sections; the knot that is made to secure the tie will disguise the seam of the front section. The tie is lined with dark blue silk habotai.

Most commercial ties are made of very thin printed silk and many are bulked out by the use of a thin wadding down the centre of the tie, which won't be necessary for this project if you choose a good-quality fabric with sufficient bulk and thickness. Any single-coloured medium-weight fabric would be suitable, but tie silk will lend an air of authenticity to the project.

Note how the qualities of the fabric have been exploited to create a strong statement.

It is actually double-sided, with a navy and pink pattern on its opposite side, which would have worked well for a more conventional tie. However, the folded pattern will become visually lost if a strongly patterned striped fabric is used; it is much better to use a plain-coloured fabric for this purpose, as this will show up the structure of the folding better. Note also how the inherent unidirectional pattern in the weave emphasizes the different directions of the folded pattern. This is an excellent example of how choice of fabric can radically influence the creation of a garment or accessory.

The folding pattern lies on the bias, so for convenience's sake, it allows the front section of the tie to maintain a continuous grain with the middle and back sections, which are joined diagonally (compare this project with the Cowrie Belt in Chapter 7.)

The tie is made using a combination of hand- and machine-stitching. It is one size, so no alterations are needed.

step-by-step method

Materials needed: tie silk, silk habotai, white pencil, set square, tacking thread, sewing thread, fabric scissors, needle.

YOU WILL NEED

▶ Tie silk

▶ Silk habotai

▶ Matching sewing thread

▶ Tacking thread

▶ Needle

▶ White pencil

▶ Fabric scissors

▶ Set square

▶ Sewing machine

For pattern see page 137.

On the WS of the tie silk fabric, mark the bias using a set square and white pencil. This will form the axis of the folding pattern. Position the pattern pieces to allow for a generous amount of fabric around the front tie section (which will be folded and thus use up more fabric than you anticipate), and also to allow for the middle and end sections of the tie to be cut on the bias.

On your bias line, mark in the dots of the folding pattern with a white pencil. The front section of the tie will be cut out of the fabric once the folds have been stitched and pressed into place.

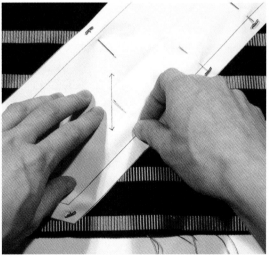

Join the dots along the axis of the folding pattern with a white pencil and the help of a set square.

Pin the middle and end-pattern pieces of the tie in position on the fabric. Align them on the bias and well away from the marked folding pattern. This will give you maximum flexibility when manipulating folds.

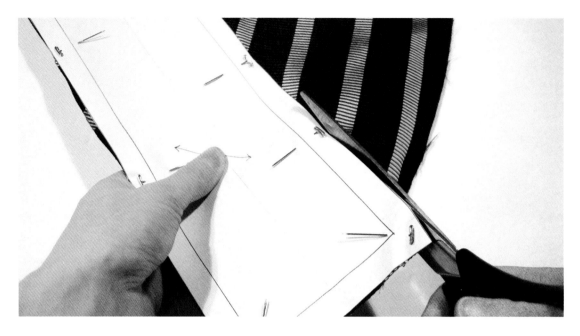

Cut out the middle and end pieces of the tie.

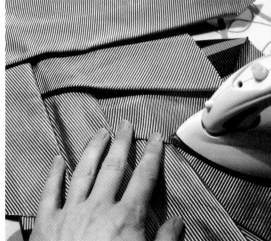

Do not cut the front section out as yet (see pattern illustration). With your needle and thread, catch two diagonally facing dots together as indicated on the pattern (from these, the fishtail folds will be created later). Work from the bottom to the top of the tie.

Turn the fabric to the RS. Fold the stitched sections into position so that the edges of the folds point downwards towards the base of the tie and they make a fishtail pattern in the manner shown. Work from the bottom to the top of the tie. Press the folds lightly and on a low to medium setting.

When pressed, tack the folded central section to hold it in position.

Mark the bias on the silk habotai lining.

Draw round the lining pieces onto the fabric using a white pencil.

Cut out the lining pieces.

middle and end sections are joined diagonally

Machine-sew the short ends of the middle and end sections of the main fabric together.

Do the same for the middle and end sections of the habotai lining.

Press open the seams of the middle and end tie silk and habotai-lining sections.

Trim any excess fabric from the seam edge.

Pin the front section paper pattern over the piece of folded fabric so that the fishtail-folded pattern runs directly up the centre. Cut round the pattern.

The folded front section.

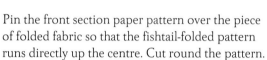

Press the edges of the front section under to a width of approximately 1 cm ($^3/_8$ in.).

Tack the turned-under edges of the front section to hold them in place.

Secure the bottom point of the tie-front section with oversewing stitches.

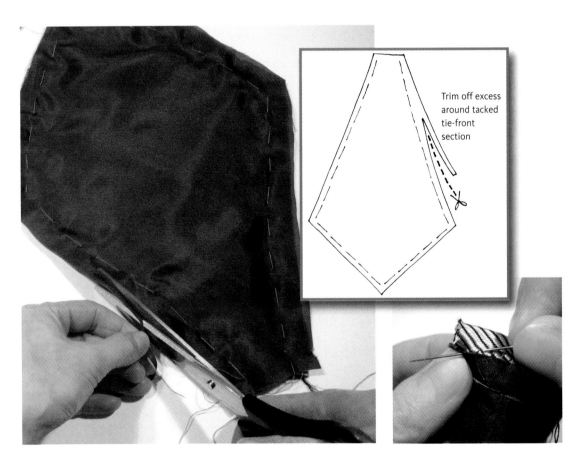

Trim off excess around tacked tie-front section

Tack the silk habotai linings to the front and end sections, as shown. Trim off any excess.

Secure the linings to the silk with hemstitching, turning the edges of the lining under as you go.

Remove the tacking.

Fold over the sides of the middle, end and front sections of the tie so that they overlap, and press.

Turn the overlap under to neaten.

Tack up the centre of both sections of the tie to secure the overlap. Stitch the edge down using hemstitch.

Stitch the side corners of the tie front section securely in place using a few catch stitches.

Insert the open end of the front section of the tie into the open end of the back section and tack the two sections together.

Turn the edge of the back section of the tie under and stitch both sections together using a hemstitch.

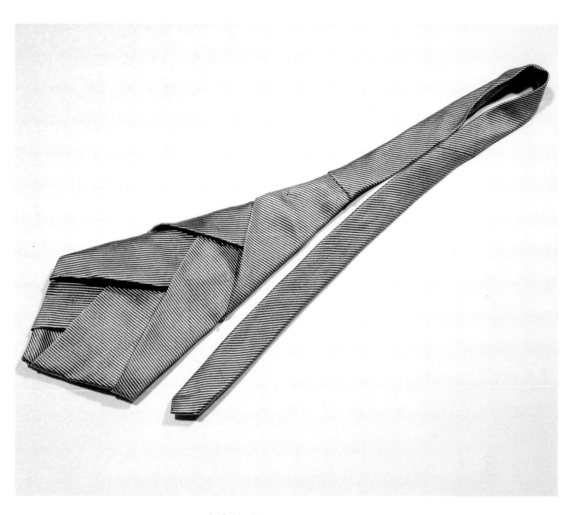

The finished tie.

12   feather collar

This decorative and glamorous collar, ideal for red-carpet or similarly opulent occasions, is made from lengths of feather trim stitched to a stiffened and wired felt base lined with silk satin and edged with petersham. The edge of the collar is covered with coordinating folded organza ribbon, and embroidered with a free-form, random pattern of blue, green, violet and gunmetal-coloured metallic and glass iridescent beads. It is close-fitting, with a toggle fastening the front, and partly covers the cheeks of the wearer.

The collar construction makes use of some techniques found in millinery, such as stabilising the edge by wiring and edging with petersham. This will give the item a degree of stability, but also flexibility. I chose felt for a base partly because it is traditionally used in hats in conjunction with the wire/petersham stabilising techniques, and found that the technique worked very well for collars of this type. Felt is also extremely easy to cut and sew,

especially in conjunction with a feather trim; its surface will be completely disguised by the decorative feather and ribbon/bead decoration. In fact, any fabric with a reasonable amount of strength and bulk, when stiffened, will provide a good base. The collar is lined with luxurious silk-satin lining cut on the bias, although acetate lining will also be suitable and probably more hard-wearing.

Use curved petersham when finishing the edge; straight petersham will not give the requisite flexibility. I would recommend petersham as an edging over bias binding or ribbon binding, since it is much tougher and the wire does not show through at the edges. It is not mandatory that you stretch the petersham on a block first (as you would for millinery), since the action of pulling it as you work, and the warmth of your hands, will also shape it. The stiffener will also need no trimming; this is due to the edges of the collar and collar lining being encased in petersham.

step-by-step method

Materials you may need: pink felt, pink silk satin for lining, firm stiffener, pliers, millinery wire, needles, matching organza ribbon, petersham (curved), fabric scissors, silk thread for tacking and sewing, fineliner, iridescent and gunmetal-effect beads, toggle, pink and iridescent-green feathers.

YOU WILL NEED

- ▸ Felt
- ▸ Silk satin (lining)
- ▸ Vilene® H250
- ▸ Organza ribbon, 3 m (3 ⅓ yd)
- ▸ Petersham (curved), 1.25 m (1 ⅚ yd)
- ▸ Green iridescent cock-feather trim, 66 cm (26 in.)

- ▸ Contrast-coloured chicken feather trim, 66 cm (26 in.)
- ▸ Matching silk thread
- ▸ Tacking thread (silk)
- ▸ Fineliner
- ▸ Tailor's chalk
- ▸ Needle
- ▸ Beading needle

- ▸ Fabric scissors
- ▸ Millinery wire, 0.3–0.5 size
- ▸ Pliers for wire cutting
- ▸ Assortment of iridescent and gunmetal-effect glass and metal beads
- ▸ Toggle, 7.5 cm (3 in.)

For pattern see page 139.

A SPECIAL NOTE ON MEASUREMENTS

Since the collar is designed to fit a specific neck measurement, you may need to construct your own pattern. I would recommend that you copy the pattern drawing of the collar to scale. The inside curve of the pattern should measure 37 cm (14½ in.) and has been designed for a 33 cm (13 in.) neck. I would advocate working with the neck measurement of the wearer plus an additional 4 cm (1½ in.) for the length of the inner curve.

To increase the measurement of the collar, project the arms of the inside curve along the curve of the circle that functions as a construction line, so that the correct measurement is achieved, then draw in the outside curve to match. If you consider that the extra length needs to be divided by two then added to either side, the pattern may not need much manipulation.

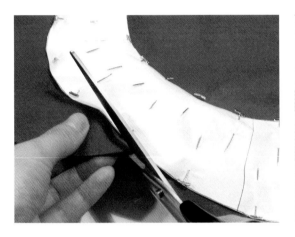

Pin the collar pattern to the felt and cut it out.

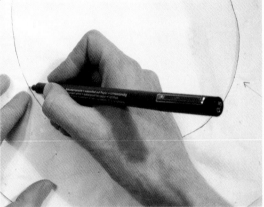

Using the collar pattern, draw round it onto the stiffener with a fineliner.

Iron the stiffener onto the felt.

Sew millinery wire around the entire edge of the collar to stiffen it, using an oversewing stitch and taking your stitches directly through the edge of the collar. Make sure that there is an overlap at the beginning of the wire, at the CB.

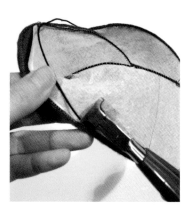

Trim any excess wire with pliers.

Hemstitch petersham 0.9 cm ($^3/_8$ in.) to 1.3 cm ($^1/_2$ in.) from the outer edge of the top of the collar, not going all the way through the fabric with the needle. Ensure there is an overlap at the end of the petersham which folds under; make this at the CB.

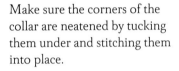

Make sure the corners of the collar are neatened by tucking them under and stitching them into place.

Cut a length of green iridescent feather trim to fit around the circumference of the collar. Tack it into place at the top of the crescent collar shape.

Trim any excess length of feather trim at either end of the crescent collar.

Machine-stitch the trim into position.

Do the same for one length of pink feather trim (positioned below the green feather trim to conceal its upper edge).

Pin and stitch organza ribbon to cover the base of the pink feather trim, doubling it over to get the effect shown.

The feather collar so far.

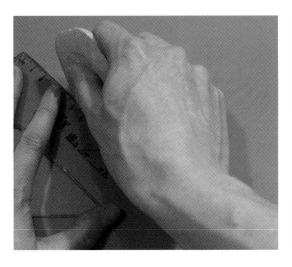

Mark pink silk satin with tailor's chalk and a set square to find the bias.

Place the collar lining pattern so that the bias aligns with the CB, then draw round it carefully with a fineliner, making sure that the fabric does not move (silk satin being notoriously mobile).

Cut out the silk-satin lining and push it gently inside the collar so that it will be concealed by the free edge of the petersham, which is about to be stitched down.

Tack the free edge of the petersham all the way around the collar to cover the lining. Take the tacking stitches all the way to the other side of the collar, through to the top edge.

Hemstitch the petersham to the lining so that the edge of the collar is neat, then remove the tacking threads.

Stitch beads onto the ribbon in a random pattern to cover the ribbon folds, using a beading needle. Make up the framework of the pattern with the large beads first, then fill in the gaps with smaller iridescent beads.

Bend the collar into a comfortable shape; this can be done easily because of the wired edge.

Attach the parts of the toggle to either end of the collar on its reverse (lined) side.

The finished collar.

13 faux fur wrap

Technically speaking, the wrap falls into the 'shawl' or 'pashmina' family of scarves, which don't so much encompass the neck as wrap around the body for warmth and comfort. Vegetarians will appreciate this eye-catching 'funky Western' wrap, which is all faux – being made of a lightweight animal-printed faux-fur fabric and assortment of brightly coloured trims, including double-sided faux-suede fringing. The wrap is lined with a vibrant pink quilted silk-satin, and can be worn in any number of ways; for example, the top part of the neck rolled over to make the fabulous contrast lining visible. Though fairly light, it is also surprisingly warm.

This item takes a little longer to make, due to the amount of machine quilting involved and accurate symmetrical placing of the trims, but is well worth the effort! You would be advised to purchase one or two of the larger reels of sewing thread, since the machine quilting will use up considerable amounts.

step-by-step method

You will need: Quiltex® fabric, pink silk satin for lining, lightweight fake-fur fabric, fabric scissors, ribbon trim, fake-suede trims, tacking thread, sewing thread, needles, tape measure.

YOU WILL NEED

- Thin, lightweight faux-fur fabric
- Pink silk satin (for lining)
- Quiltex® (Vilene® X50)
- Sewing thread (choose a colour that harmonizes with some aspects of the wrap and contrasts with others)

- Tacking thread
- Needle
- Tape measure
- Fabric scissors
- 'Ethnic' ribbon trim, 5 cm (2 in.) wide

- Fake-suede bicoloured fringing trims, 9 cm (3½ in.) wide

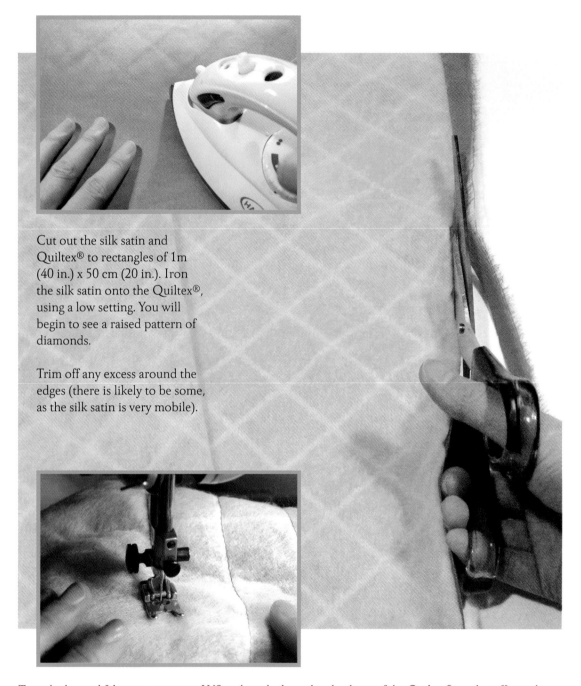

Cut out the silk satin and
Quiltex® to rectangles of 1m
(40 in.) x 50 cm (20 in.). Iron
the silk satin onto the Quiltex®,
using a low setting. You will
begin to see a raised pattern of
diamonds.

Trim off any excess around the
edges (there is likely to be some,
as the silk satin is very mobile).

Turn the layered fabric over onto its WS and stitch along the glue lines of the Quiltex®, so that effectively,
you are stitching the fabric upside down. Stitching on the WS is easier to see than if it were done on the RS.
I also find that the needle will not pierce the 'satin' side of the silk-satin fabric (on which long weft threads
float) as easily as the opposite side, and thus snagging of the fabric will be avoided.

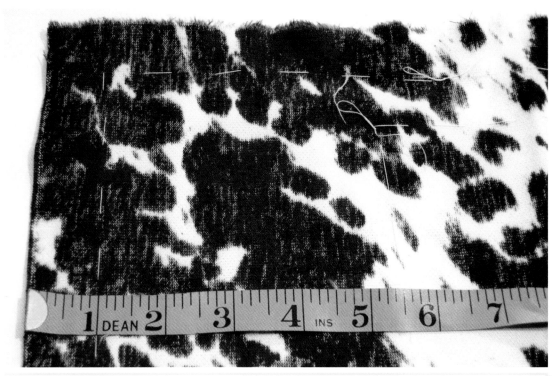

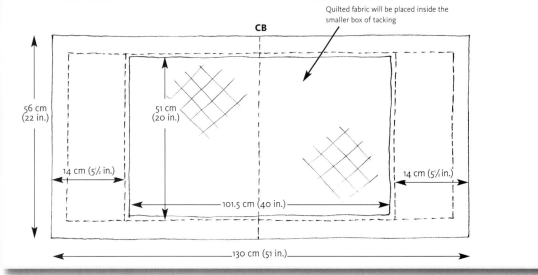

Quilted fabric will be placed inside the smaller box of tacking

CB

56 cm (22 in.)

51 cm (20 in.)

14 cm (5½ in.)

14 cm (5½ in.)

101.5 cm (40 in.)

130 cm (51 in.)

Cut out the fake-fur fabric to dimensions of 130 cm (51 in.) x 56 cm (22 in.). There will be a generous turnover at the sides, approx. 28 cm (11 in.) in total, and also at the upper and lower edges 5 cm (2 in.) in total; this will serve partly as a facing. Mark the positions of the turnovers and quilted lining with lines of tacking 2.5 cm (1 in.) all round the edges and 14 cm (5½ in.) in from the sides as shown in the drawing; find the CB by folding or measuring, and also mark that with a line of tacking.

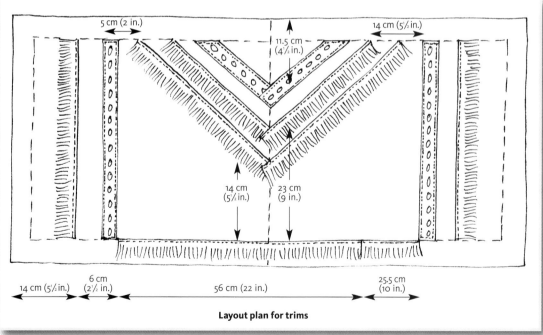

5 cm (2 in.)

14 cm (5½ in.)

11.5 cm
(4½ in.)

14 cm
(5½ in.)

23 cm
(9 in.)

14 cm (5½ in.)

6 cm
(2½ in.)

56 cm (22 in.)

25.5 cm
(10 in.)

Layout plan for trims

On the right side of the fabric, tack the trims into position as shown in the drawing above. Turn under the short edges of the patterned ribbon trim, but not those of the fake-suede trims.

Stitch all the trims into position using matching or contrasting thread.

To make a 'V' in the pattern at the CB, simply overlap two sections of trim in the manner shown.

Place and pin the quilted lining into position inside the smaller 'box' of tacked stitches.

Handstitch the lining into position using a hemstitch/blindstitch that is not visible from the RS of the fur fabric.

Fold over the sides of the wrap to make a generous facing, so that the fake-suede trim along the shorter edges forms an edging to either side. Pin and tack all around the edges of the folds.

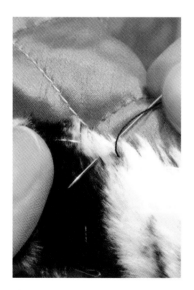

Secure the hems thus created with hemstitches.

Secure the free edges at each corner of the wrap with a small and imperceptible oversewing stitch.

opposite The finished wrap, with pattern detail shown.

14 designing your own accessories

We can think of scarves, collars, ties and belts taking as their pattern basis a long rectangular strip of fabric. This is a relatively uncomplicated place from which to start when compared with other fashion items, and makes the design process comparatively easy. It also allows for a great deal of interpretation in terms of shape, fabric manipulation and decoration.

As can be seen from the examples within this book, which offer just a flavour of the potential within this area of design, the rectangular strip can be modified through cutting and shaping into more sophisticated lines; decorative cutting in order to sculpt the fabric, as with felt; decorating with feathers, beads, buckles, rhinestones and trims; using fasteners as decorative elements within the design; using different fabric combinations and fabric qualities to enhance the design of the accessory; quilting, tucking, and folding fabric to alter its shape, visual appearance, feel and texture. This book offers an opportunity to try out all these techniques, and demonstrates how they can be used to make simple and effective accessories within a relatively short time frame. Experiment by making an accessory using an alternative fabric, or by using a specific technique to make an altogether different accessory. For example, the technique used to make the 'ruched-effect' base of the Polka Dot Collar in chapter 10 could be applied with great effect to making a belt.

This chapter will deal mainly with basic pattern-cutting as applied to the accessories in this book. The simple skills shown here can be transferred to any subsequent accessories project of your choice. The patterns in this book can be manipulated as much as you like through pattern cutting and choice of decoration, although the original designs themselves are for personal use only. I haven't included a large design-inspirations section, as the subject is covered extensively elsewhere, and I also find that inspiration and the ability to realise a design tends to grow alongside confidence in one's own pattern-cutting skills. You will need paper and at the very least a pencil, Sellotape® and paper scissors to try out the exercises in this chapter.

how cutting affects the shape and fit

YOU WILL NEED

- Propelling pencil
- Drafting or putty eraser
- Fineliner pen
- Ruler (marked in both inches and centimetres if possible)

- Set square
- Protractor
- Compasses
- French curves
- Flexible curve

- Layout paper (semi-transparent, good for pattern-drafting)
- Thin card (optional, for making master patterns)
- Paper scissors
- Sellotape®

It is interesting to note how a basic pattern shape used for many soft accessory patterns changes with the type of item, its choice of material, and its use. A simple belt, collar or scarf starts out as a rectangular strip; however, this may be changed through cutting and spreading of the pattern to provide a better fit.

This is where basic pattern-cutting skills come in. Cut a rectangular strip from a length of paper. Fold it along its length and then back on itself; this will reduce the length equally along both sides. This technique can be used either to reduce the length of the pattern, or a tuck can be plotted at this position. (To increase the length of the pattern, see below.)

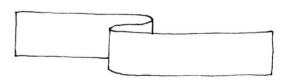

Or make the width of the fold unequal on both sides. You will see how the length of the strip is reduced and how, when folds of unequal width are made, a curve is formed along one side or another.

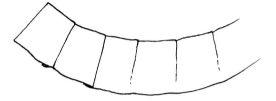

The free (as opposed to folded) part of the curve will retain its original length, but the length of the folded side will be reduced considerably.

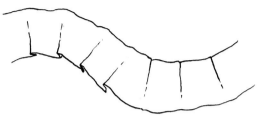

The effects of an unequal width of fold on both sides of the material.

Cut another rectangular strip. Divide it into 2.5 cm (1 in.) sections. Now, cut down these sections, working from one side to the other. Do not cut all the way to the other side. Place the strip carefully on a fresh sheet of paper. Working one section at a time, use tape to secure each section onto this sheet of paper. You will observe that each section can be moved independently of the last section. Tape down the sections so that there is 2.5 cm (1 in.) between the corners of adjacent sections on their free sides. (To increase the length of the pattern shape equally along both sides, make the distance between the sections equal on both sides, as opposed to one.)

2.5 cm (1 in.)

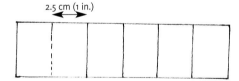

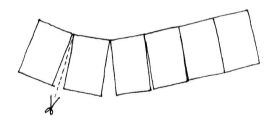

Divide a rectangular strip into 2.5 cm (1 in.) equal sections, cutting each section almost to the other side.

When all the sections are taped down, this will give you the basis for your pattern shape. To refine the shape of the pattern, take your propelling pencil and, using the placement of the sections as a guide, draw a curve that links all the sections. You may find it useful to use your French curves or flexible curve rather than work freehand, in order to create a curve that is pleasing to the eye; going over your lines with a fineliner will also better define the shape. This type of cutting, called 'cut and spread', will ensure that one side of the item retains its original length; however, the opposite side will be increased in length. The distances between sections can be manipulated according to the desired effect.

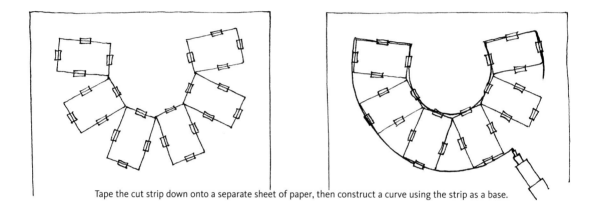

Tape the cut strip down onto a separate sheet of paper, then construct a curve using the strip as a base.

From having applied this method of cutting we can see how the original rectangular strip pattern has metamorphosed into a pattern which curves along both sides. These types of curves may fit the body better and provide a more pleasing shape than a simple strip, depending of course on the choice and bias orientation of material.

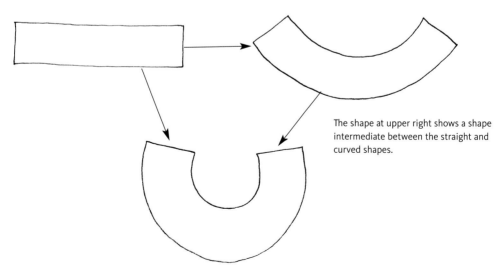

The shape at upper right shows a shape intermediate between the straight and curved shapes.

The metamorphosis of a straight strip into a curved shape.

When making a symmetrical item, always fold the preliminary pattern along a longitudinal axis (and, if possible, the corresponding axis at right angles to this axis) to check that it is perfectly symmetri-cal. Use your set squares and rulers to do this. It is better to check inconsistencies at this stage than find them revealed later!

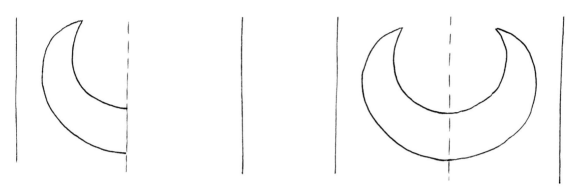

Drawing one half of the design, then tracing the mirror-image on to the other half of the paper.

The Feather Collar in chapter 12 shows another metamorphosis of the original strip shape: here the curved strip has changed into a crescent. In actual fact, although the shape could in theory have been constructed from cut and spread techniques, the crescent was constructed using com-passes, French curves, and knowledge of the neck measurement; I added a couple of inches to improve the fit. In the event that the collar in chapter 12 is not large enough, the pattern pieces can be increased in size according to instructions in that chapter.

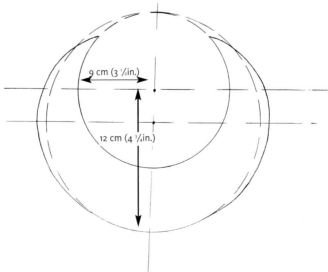

9 cm (3 ½in.)

12 cm (4 ¾in.)

Construction of the feather collar, using two circles as the guideline.

The sides of a tie are folded inwards, with one side overlapping the other, and stitched down. This is reflected in the outer fabric pattern and lining patterns of the tie in this book. Generally, continuous angles of 45 degrees are formed from the central front point in commercial ties, but the pattern in this book dispenses with this due to the nature of the folding pattern and the width of the tie, which is greater than it would conventionally be.

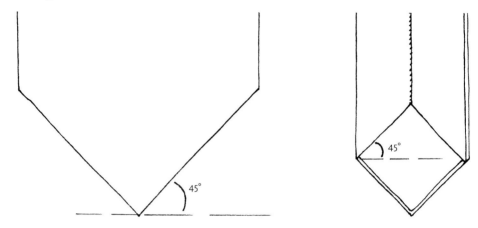

The pattern of a tie, showing how the edges are folded under to create a 'diamond' window of lining on the reverse side.

Experiment with different shapes to get an idea of how they work with the body. Assuming you are happy with the shape you have produced, cut it out with paper scissors and place it on another sheet of paper. Draw round the shape; once removed, the shape of the pattern should again be checked and any 'lumps and bumps' eliminated.

Finally, add seam allowance. Cut the pattern out using paper scissors. The pattern should now be ready to use.

The pattern can then be annotated with its name or part in the design, the type of fabric used, and the number of pieces needed.

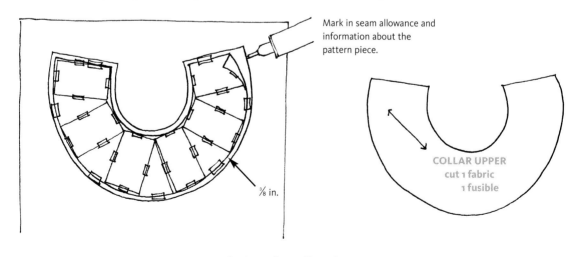

Mark in seam allowance and information about the pattern piece.

⅜ in.

COLLAR UPPER
cut 1 fabric
1 fusible

Cutting and spreading a shape.

You may want to make a master pattern from thin card if you are particularly happy with it and want to use it over a long period of time. However, I prefer thin paper patterns as they are more flexible and can be more easily fitted to the wearer, allowing for changes to be made if necessary. Grain orientation is as important in the making of soft accessories as it is with any other fashion item. If the article is intended to drape well or fit snugly round the body it should be cut on the bias; the direction of the bias should be marked with a set square at 45 degrees to the centre front (and/or centre back) line. Bias-cut lining will also help to dispense with loose or hanging areas and give the fabric more movement with the body, as opposed to a feeling of tightness. The ribbon binding used for the Folded Ribbon Tie in chapter 5 is in any case cut on the bias; using fabric on the straight grain, where it has not been manipulated, will result in the fabric taking greater precedence over the shape of the body, and give a more sculptural effect (see chapter 8, Indian Scarf).

design drawings and inspiration

In an industrial setting it is normal to create design drawings and specification sheets with attached fabric swatches. Spec sheets are detailed drawings which give an indication of the scale of the item, its style and collection names, and the details of its construction, such as the method of sewing. For example, the manufacturer might need to sew both WSS together at a certain point, or both RSS; they might need to make a single, double, zigzag or overlock seam. Typically, much of this information is presented in a box to one side of the drawing. If making items on an industrial scale it would be standard practice to provide the manufacturer with this type of drawing.

The more artistic 'design' illustrations are what are better known and appreciated by the general public. These again show the item in detail, but without the numerical specifications that characterize the spec sheet. Design drawings vary in standard; in practice they can range from highly finished artworks to drawings done on the back of a cigarette packet! As a designer it is fairly important to have drawing skills adequate enough to illustrate your work

Fashion drawing of the Indian Scarf in chapter 8
The drawing was made from a photograph using a propelling pencil, and the scarf coloured in marker pens, then worked over again in pencil to emphasize patterns and textures.

to others (including customers), and good practice to present them professionally, either in a portfolio or presentation case. Practice putting your ideas onto paper whenever you can; fine-liner or disposable technical drawing pens give a crisp and professional feel. Try to impart a sense of the worn shape and hang of the item, as well as the material with which it is constructed.

There are a number of books which cover design adequately and quite comprehensively, and space unfortunately limits the opportunities for addressing the subject in detail here. In brief, design inspirations can vary enormously and are by their very nature intensely personal. I myself would recommend the absolute beginner to start from a materials- or practically-oriented-standpoint. This is extremely helpful as it gives one a sound base from which to develop an individual style and materials preference. Looking to fashion magazines and shops for inspiration, blending those inspirations with one's own fabric and pattern ideas, then creating an item from these inspirations, is also useful as it enables one to gain construction knowledge through interpretation of basic fashionable shapes, with the potential to adapt and develop these shapes further according to resources. In the majority of situations, I would suggest that beginners start with a technical and/or decorative approach, rather than a conceptual, 'ideas'-based, 'fine art' approach; this can come later, when construction knowledge is sounder.

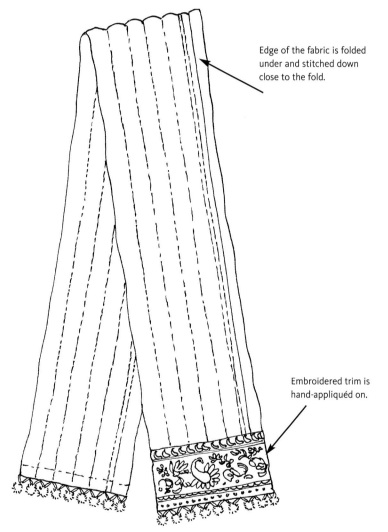

Edge of the fabric is folded under and stitched down close to the fold.

Embroidered trim is hand-appliquéd on.

patterns

Eyelet Belt

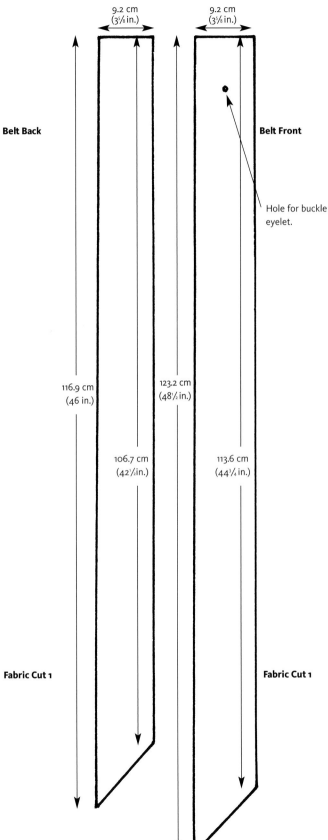

Belt Back

Belt Front

9.2 cm
(3⅝ in.)

9.2 cm
(3⅝ in.)

Hole for buckle
eyelet.

116.9 cm
(46 in.)

123.2 cm
(48½ in.)

106.7 cm
(42½ in.)

113.6 cm
(44¾ in.)

Fabric Cut 1

Fabric Cut 1

Pompom Scarf

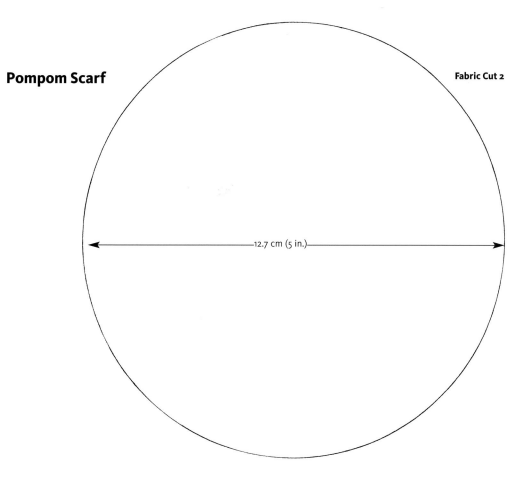

Fabric Cut 2

12.7 cm (5 in.)

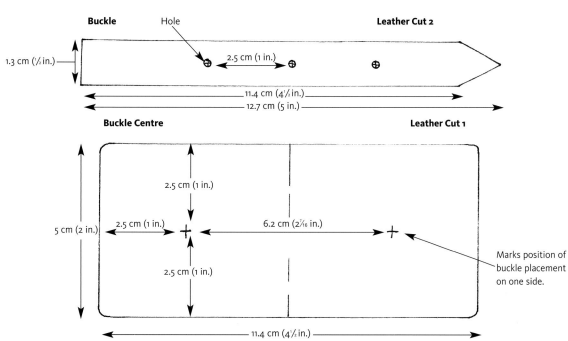

Buckle   Hole   **Leather Cut 2**

1.3 cm (½ in.)

2.5 cm (1 in.)

11.4 cm (4½ in.)

12.7 cm (5 in.)

Buckle Centre   **Leather Cut 1**

2.5 cm (1 in.)

5 cm (2 in.)   2.5 cm (1 in.)   6.2 cm (2⁷⁄₁₆ in.)

2.5 cm (1 in.)

Marks position of
buckle placement
on one side.

11.4 cm (4½ in.)

Cowrie Belt

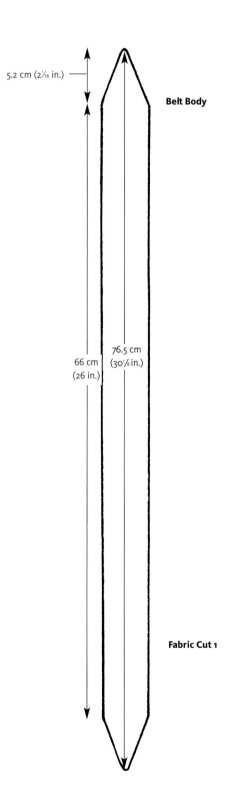

5.2 cm (2¹⁄₁₆ in.)

Belt Body

76.5 cm (30¹⁄₈ in.)

66 cm (26 in.)

Fabric Cut 1

Bollywood Belt   **Belt Front**

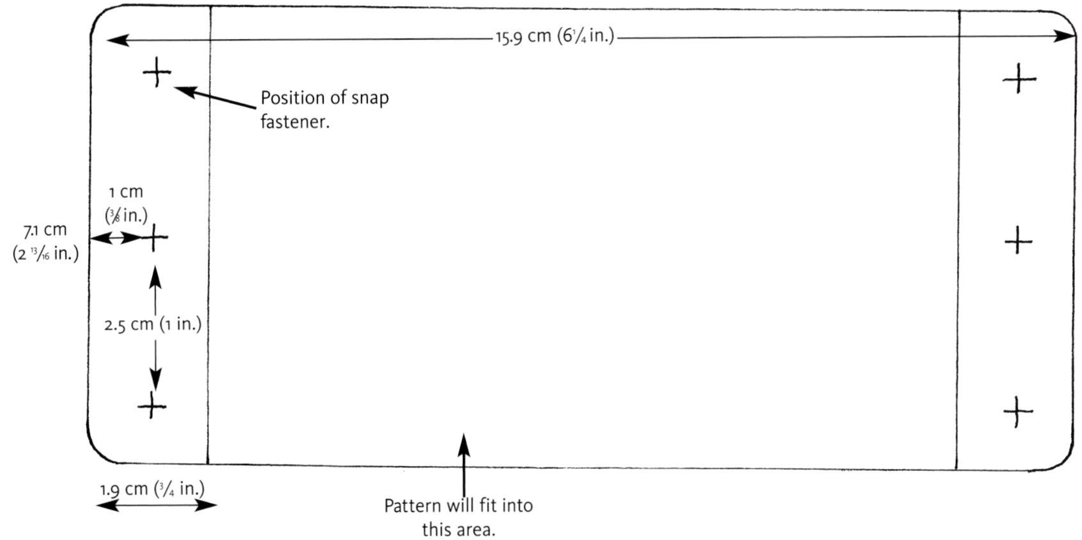

15.9 cm (6¼ in.)

Position of snap fastener.

1 cm (⅜ in.)

7.1 cm (2 ¹³⁄₁₆ in.)

2.5 cm (1 in.)

1.9 cm (¾ in.)

Pattern will fit into this area.

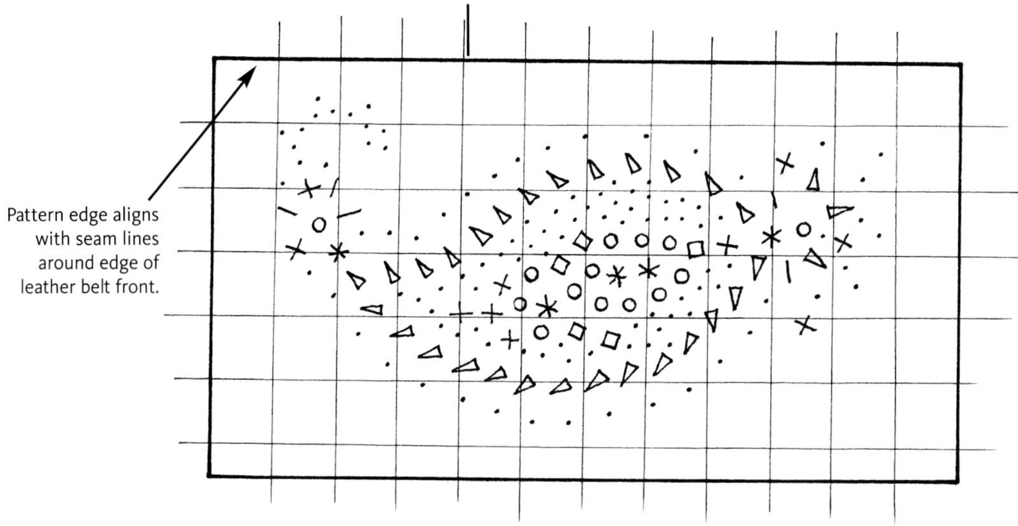

Pattern edge aligns with seam lines around edge of leather belt front.

Rhinestone Design

▢	blue opaque round, 5 mm (¼ in.)
○	orange transparent round, 5 mm (¼ in.)
✕	amber transparent round, 5 mm (¼ in.)
✱	pearlescent round, 5 mm (¼ in.)
△	pearlescent round, 5 mm (¼ in.)
╎	teardrop shape
•	leaf shape
	pearlescent round, 3 mm (⅛ in.)

Squares in grid measure 1 cm x 1 cm
(⅜ in. x ⅜ in.)

Polka Dot Collar

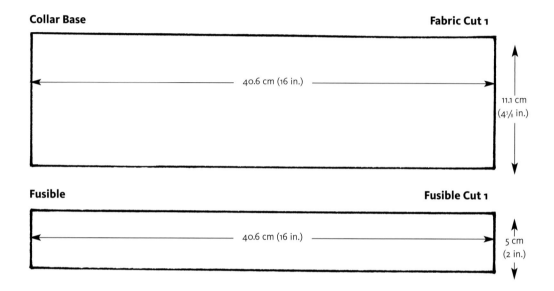

Collar Base   **Fabric Cut 1**

40.6 cm (16 in.)

11.1 cm
(4⅜ in.)

Fusible   **Fusible Cut 1**

40.6 cm (16 in.)

5 cm
(2 in.)

Folded Silk Tie 1

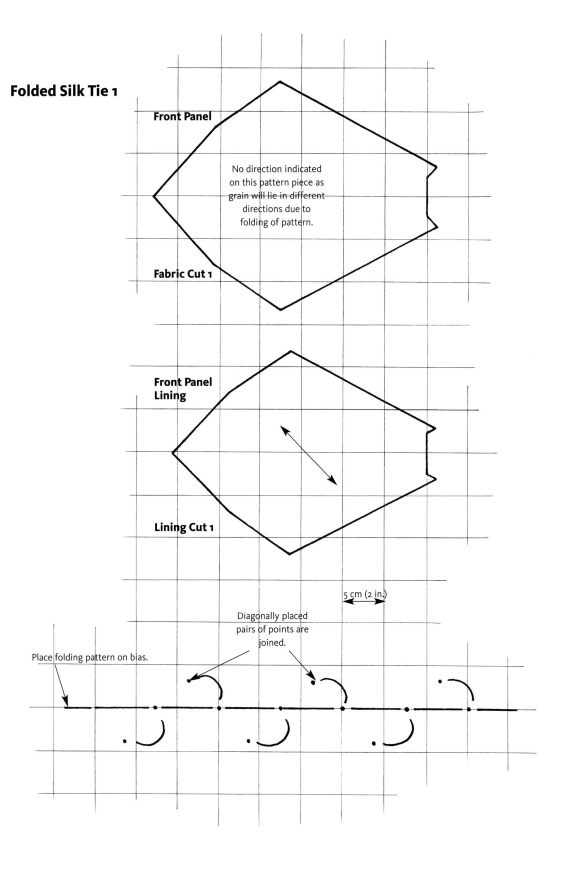

Front Panel

No direction indicated on this pattern piece as grain will lie in different directions due to folding of pattern.

Fabric Cut 1

Front Panel Lining

Lining Cut 1

5 cm (2 in.)

Diagonally placed pairs of points are joined.

Place folding pattern on bias.

Folded Silk Tie 2

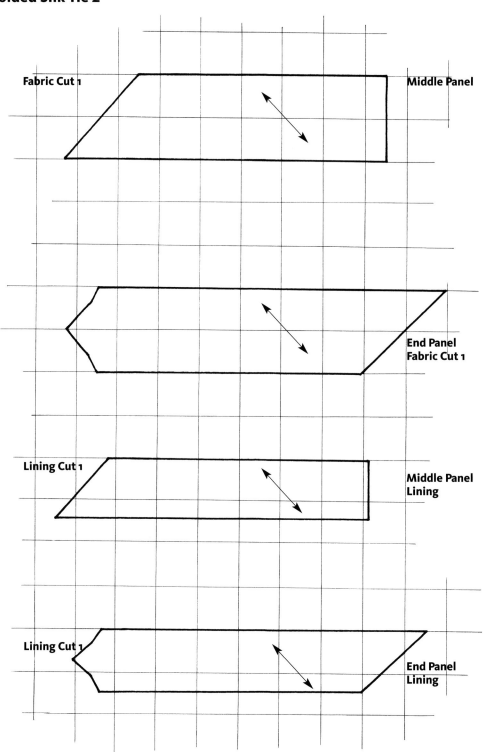

Fabric Cut 1

Middle Panel

End Panel
Fabric Cut 1

Lining Cut 1

Middle Panel
Lining

Lining Cut 1

End Panel
Lining

Feather Collar

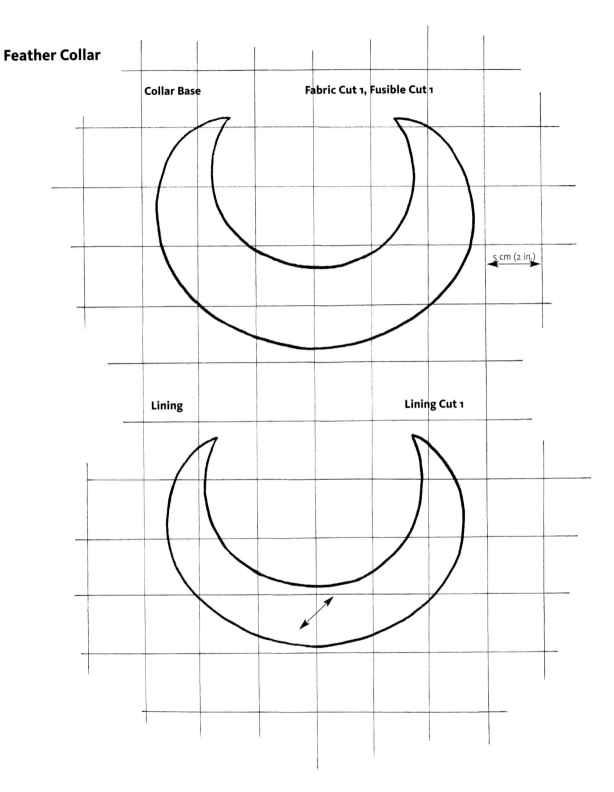

Collar Base　　　　**Fabric Cut 1, Fusible Cut 1**

5 cm (2 in.)

Lining　　　　**Lining Cut 1**

glossary

Many of the terms are already covered in chapter 2; however, here is a list of items that may be unfamiliar or are specific to accessory making and pattern construction.

Benares brocade – a brocade fabric of silk and metal-covered viscose, usually in a single bright colour, with brocade in a single metallic colour, either silver or gold. Used to make Indian jackets and saris.

Circle template – a piece of drawing equipment with circles of varying sizes, useful for positioning buckle holes and drawing curved corners in pattern drafting.

Cover buttons – buttons which can be covered with self-fabric.

French curves – drawing implements with a variety of shaped curves in varying sizes that are useful for pattern-drafting.

Fusibles – fabrics coated with glue on one or both sides that give stability to outer fabrics and are fixed by ironing.

Layout paper – thin semi-transparent paper useful for sketching, pattern-making and drafting.

Petersham – a type of braid used in millinery for the edges of hats; the curved, rather than straight, petersham can be pulled or steamed into shape to fit the edge of the item better.

Quiltex® – trade name for a type of Vilene® whose reverse side is coated in a heat-fixable glue in a diamond pattern, and which, together with a fabric of your choice, can be used to create a quilted composite fabric.

RS – right side.

RSS – right sides.

Style line – a line along which the pattern is cut, which also has a decorative function.

Vilene® – trade name for a variety of fusibles of different types, defined by number.

Wire, millinery – paper- or thread-covered wire used in millinery in order to shape the edges of hats, and also suitable for more theatrical accessories when used in conjunction with petersham.

WS – wrong side.

WSS – wrong sides.

bibliography

This is a brief list of books that may be interesting from the point of view of pattern-cutting, construction or design:

Aldrich, Winifred, *Fabric, Form and Flat Pattern Cutting*, pub. Blackwell Science Ltd, 1996, ISBN 0-632-03917-5.
(pattern-cutting)

Evans, Deborah (ed.), *The Hamlyn Complete Sewing Course*, pub. Hamlyn Publishing Group Ltd, 1989, ISBN 0-600-564495-9.
(sewing, construction)

Grant, Catherine (ed.), *New Directions in Jewellery*, pub. Black Dog Publishing Ltd, 2005, ISBN 1-904772-19-6
(design, inspiration, particularly from fabric-jewellery design perspective)

Hart, Avril, *Ties*, pub. V & A Publications, 1998, ISBN 1851772251
(history, design, inspiration)

stockists

Most of the suppliers of fabric used in this book are located within London's West End (nearest tubes: Oxford St, Tottenham Court Rd, Bond St, Piccadilly Circus) and are within easy walking distance of each other. Where possible websites and email addresses have also been provided.

Barnett Lawson Trimmings, 16–17 Little Portland St, London W1W 8NE (wholesalers): mock suede fringing for Faux Fur Wrap, chapter 13.
Tel: 020 7636 8591
Email: info@bltrimmings.com
www.bltrimmings.com

Berwick St Cloth Shop, 14 Berwick St, London W1F 0PP: faux-fur fabric for Faux Fur Wrap, chapter 13.
Tel: 020 7287 2881
Email: berwickstcloth@aol.com
www.thesilksociety.com

Borovick Fabrics Ltd, 16 Berwick St, London W1F 0HP: leather pieces for Pompom Scarf, chapter 6; Bollywood Belt, chapter 9; denim for Eyelet Belt, chapter 4.
Tel: 020 7437 2180
Email: borovickfabrics@btclick.com
www.borovickfabricsltd.co.uk.

Broadwick Silks, 9–11 Broadwick St, London W1F 0DB: Benares brocade for Cowrie Belt, chapter 7.
Tel: 020 7734 3320
Email: broadwicksilks@aol.com
www.thesilksociety.com

Cloth House, 47 Berwick St, London W1F 8SJ, also 98 Berwick St, London W1F 0QJ: felt for Felt Boa, chapter 3; wool fabric for Pompom Scarf, chapter 6; Indian print fabric and trims for Indian Scarf, chapter 8; tie silk for Folded Tie, chapter 11; felt for Feather Collar, chapter 12; silk satin lining for Faux Fur Wrap, chapter 13.
Tel: 020 7485 6247
Email: info@clothhouse.com

Creative Beadcraft, 20 Beak St, London W1F 9RE: sew-on rhinestones for Eyelet Belt, chapter 4; rhinestones for Bollywood Belt, chapter 9; seed beads and thong for Cowrie Belt, chapter 7; beads for Feather Collar, chapter 12.
Tel: 020 7629 9964
Email: tracey@creativebeadcraft.co.uk
www.creative-beadcraft.co.uk.

MacCulloch & Wallis, 25–26 Dering St, London W1S 1AT: belt buckle and eyelets for Eyelet Belt, chapter 4; ribbon binding for Folded Ribbon Tie, chapter 5; faux-fur trim for Pompom Scarf, chapter 6; snap fasteners for Bollywood Belt, chapter 9; cover button for Polka Dot Collar, chapter 10; silk habotai lining for Folded Tie, chapter 11; feather and ribbon trims for Feather Collar, chapter 12; fusible stiffeners and wadding, also millinery wire.
Tel: 020 7629 0311
Email: macculloch@psilink.co.uk
www.macculloch-wallis.co.uk

Milliner Warehouse, 35 Ebury Bridge Rd, London SW1W 8QX: Millinery wire for Feather Collar, chapter 12.
Tel: 020 730 4918
Email: info@millinerwarehouse.com
www.millinerwarehouse.co.uk

index